KU-493-542

ESCAPE TO THE SEA

he Elaine *at anchor, Ala Moona*

ESCAPE
TO THE SEA

The adventures of
FRED REBELL

*who sailed single-handed in an
open boat 9,000 miles across the
Pacific in search of happiness*

with an Introduction by
RICHARD HUGHES

*

JOHN MURRAY
ALBEMARLE STREET
LONDON

First Edition . . . *1939*
Reprinted *1951*

C 61288 209

HERTFORDSHIRE
COUNTY LIBRARY
734493
910·4

Printed in Great Britain by D. R. Hillman & Co., Frome

CONTENTS

PART I   FRED REBELL IS BORN

CHAPTER I

Escape from Russia—A Second-hand Passport—" Fred Rebell " is Born—How to Treat Lunatics—Stowaway to Australia—A Settler on the Land

CHAPTER II

Wanted, a Wife—Lonie—The Great War—A Friendless Girl—Marriage—Paulie—The Amorous Engine-driver—I become a Carpenter—A Divorce—A New Love

CHAPTER III

Elaine—Her Beauty and Her Shortcomings—True Love at Last—Rejection—A Broken Heart—Damp-proofing

CHAPTER IV

The Great Depression—On the Dole—Thoughts of Suicide—A New Plan—My Boast to the Consul—I Buy a Boat—The Elaine Described—Fitting Out—I Make a Sextant—My " Chronometers "—I Make a Taffrail Log—Study Seamanship—Draw my Charts—Passport Trouble—Again a Matter of Conscience

PART II   THE VOYAGE

CHAPTER V

Departure from Sydney—A " Buster "—The Two School-boys—Seasickness—" Good-bye, Australia ! "—Elaine Sails Herself—I Jettison My Mandolin—Dirty Weather in the

CONTENTS

Tasman Sea—An Improvised Sea-anchor—A Leak—A Novel Leak-alarm—I Mend the Leak—Longitude Computation—Four Weeks at Sea—I Miss New Zealand—I Mend a Watch

CHAPTER VI

In the Tropics—Approaching Fiji—My First Prayer—Nearing Land—Disaster Averted—A Puzzling Problem—The Voice in the Night

CHAPTER VII

I Land for the First Time—The Rocking Earth—The Chinese Schooner—Natives—The Bar of Nature—Native Cooking—I Join the Dance—The Market—The Fire-Walkers of Mbengga.

CHAPTER VIII

Arrival at Suva—Three-headed Cerberus—The Fiji Times—Fame: Her Pros and Cons—A Merry Picnic—A Bewitching Maiden—Fijian Economy—The Stranglehold of Tariffs—The Straits of a Chieftain—" Malua Fever "—I Learn My Punishment—April 20th : to Sea Again

CHAPTER IX

Night Sailing in Narrow Waters—Saved by a Dream—The " Date Line "—Arrival at Naitamba—A Hospitable Planter —Eden with Three Eves—Another Picnic—Gentle Betty—I Run Away to Sea

CHAPTER X

The Fijis Left Behind—Gales and Head Winds—The Lost Infant—Fish and Birds—May 24th : Arrival at Apia (Samoa)—Native Society To-day—The Mau Movement—The New Zealand Mandate—Tariffs Again

CONTENTS

CHAPTER XI

Samoa—Diseases and Pests Introduced from Abroad—
" Gone Native "—A Belgian Beach-comber—A Samoan
Princess—The Native Point of View—Stevenson's Grave—
A Lovely Little Half-caste—The Importance of Shaving—
Farewell, Samoa !

CHAPTER XII

June 25th : Danger Islands—A Tiny Community—Seventh
Day Adventism—Laxity of Morals—Communal Economy—
A Malthusian Riddle—A Melancholy Impression—A Long
Passage Ahead—Telling the Time by Jarvis Island—
Navigating by the Flight of Birds—A Curious Dream—
Logarithms for Breakfast—Waterspouts—I Fall Ill—
August 14th : Approaching Christmas Island

CHAPTER XIII

Jostled by Sharks—Currents—A Charming French Planter
—Half a Million Coconut Palms—A Plague of Black Cats—
Dogs that Catch Sharks—Mutton-birds—I Make Myself a
Passport—M. Rougier Visas it—August 25th : to Sea Again
—The Doldrums—Squalls—The N.E. Trades at Last—The
Booby and the Frigate-bird—September 15th : Hawaii
Sighted—Arrival at Honolulu

CHAPTER XIV

Description of Honolulu—My Home-made Passport—
Visiting the Island Sights—Youthful Imitators—A Discussion
on Religion—Navigation by Dream—A Comparison with
the Homing Instinct of Birds—November 3rd : Good-bye
to Honolulu—A Long Lap : A Three-thousand mile Passage
Ahead

CONTENTS

CHAPTER XV

My Watches Prove Unreliable—Reading and Meditation—A December Cyclone—The Sea-anchor Fails—Cross-seas—On her Beam-ends—" I am in Trouble, Birdie ! "—The Centre-board as Drogue—Wells or the Bible—Prayer—The Gale Moderates—Lovely Sailing Weather—My Thoughts Fly to Lady-fancies—I Lose all Knowledge of my Longitude—Christmas at Sea—Another Gale—Disbelief is Elastic—New Year's Day, 1933—Prayer Answered Again—Why it did not Convince Me—A Vision—January 3rd : the Coast of America Sighted—The Lamp—Becalmed—January 8th, 1933, My Voyage Ends

PART III   THE AFTERMATH

CHAPTER XVI

Los Angeles—Red Tape—" The Regulations are Lousy ! "—Publicity—I Refuse to Lecture—Elaine Wrecked in Harbour—The Immigration Department—Cunning Questions—Harry Pidgeon—I am Arrested—Graft in the Immigration Department—How the Wretched Immigrant is Bled—Behind Bars—Released on Recognizances

CHAPTER XVII

California—Multiplicity of Sects—Hollywood—The Use of Publicity—An Earthquake—I Join the " Holy Rollers "—How I Earned My Living—Talk with the Preacher

CHAPTER XVIII

Two and a Half Years in California : My Boast Fulfilled—Arrested Again—The Deportation Barracks—American Prisons—Sex Perversion and Religiosity—Deported from the United States—My Home-coming—Nostalgia for the Pacific—" Go, Little Book ! "

ILLUSTRATIONS

Facing
page

The " Elaine " at anchor, Ala Moana . Frontispiece

A West Australian feller chopping off a kari treetop .   13

Home-made navigating instruments   .   .   .   34

The author taking a sight   36

Trying out the boat in harbour   36

Suva military band   88

The heights, Island of Naitamba .   .   .   88

The camping-hut   134
     By courtesy of the Bishop Museum

The Pandanus palm   134
     By courtesy of the Bishop Museum

A home-made passport   160

Two single-handed sailors : Harry Pidgeon and the
    author at San Pedro, California, 1933   .   .   218
     Photo by Stanley Wheeler : " Los Angeles Herald and Express "

Digging the " Elaine " out of sand   .   .   .   218

Track-chart of author's voyage   vii

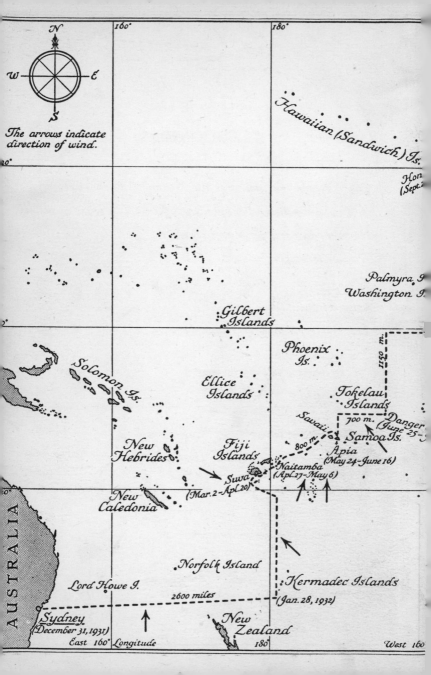

140°

Los Angeles
(January 8, 1933)

2400 miles

Hurricane

Kanai
Oahu
Maui

Hawaii

1300 miles

Fanning Island
Christmas Island
(Aug. 15-25)

Jarvis Island
(July 31)

Equator

120°

Marquesas Islands

land
ly 7)

Wallis Islands

Savaii
Apia
Upola
Tutu
American Sam

Futuna

SAMOA ISLANDS

Vanua Levu

Nanuku Passage

Naitamba

Kora
Koro Sea

Uti Levu
Suva
Yanutha
Naselai Lighthouse
Mbengga

FIJI ISLANDS

Kandavu Passage

INTRODUCTION

" FRED REBELL " here describes one of the most
extraordinary feats of single-handed sailing ever
attempted. He says he has sailed nine thousand
miles across the Pacific, from Sydney to Los Angeles,
in an eighteen-foot racing-boat, with only a canvas
hood for shelter. The voyage lasted a year and a
week. No other comparable single-handed voyage
in a small *cabinless* boat is known to history.

When he set out he apparently knew nothing
about sailing, except what he had read in Sydney
Public Library. His charts were pencil copies made
from an out-of-date atlas, from which whole archi-
pelagoes were missing. His chronometers were a
pair of cheap watches. His sextant he made himself
from pieces of hoop-iron and a hack-saw blade, with
bits of stainless steel table-knife for mirrors. His
patent log was based on an alarm-clock, converted to
read in sea-miles. For he was on the dole. Ship,
instruments, stores for a year—his *total* expenditure
was £45.

*   *   *

Let me recall one or two of the classic voyages

that have been made in small vessels, to show wherein this one differed from all the others.

First, Captain Joshua Slocum : he was the father of them. He was a Nova Scotian : a mariner all his life, and a Master Mariner for the greater part of it : but the advent of steam presently left him (as it left so many other fine captains) without a command. For a year or two he was high and dry. Then, in 1892, he was presented (as a rather unkind joke) with the remains of an old sloop, the *Spray*, fast disintegrating in a meadow near New Bedford. He rebuilt her with his own hands : had one unsuccessful season as a fisherman : and in 1895 set out on what was probably the first of the great single-handed voyages in recorded history. For Captain Slocum ultimately sailed the *Spray* alone round the world.

First he crossed the North Atlantic to Gibraltar, in the very fast time of twenty-nine days, intending to pass on eastwards through the Mediterranean. But the menace of Moorish pirates (one chased him, but was fortunately dismasted by a squall) made him reverse his decision ; he now decided to go westabout, and set sail from Gibraltar for Cape Horn. There he was again held up by a series of contrary gales so protracted that he changed his mind a second time, and prepared to sail for the Cape of Good Hope—eastabout once more ! But just then the weather at last relented, and he passed through into the Pacific : and so at last made his circumnavigation westabout after all.

This voyage was a magnificent piece of seamanship ; and Captain Slocum's book about it, *Sailing Alone Round the World*, is one of the classics of its kind ; as terse and lively to-day as when it was written.

What became of Captain Slocum in the end nobody knows : he disappeared at sea, and is believed to have been run down in a fog.

Now these are the points to bear in mind about Slocum's voyage. He himself was a fine seaman, a professional, more at home at sea than on shore. The *Spray*, too, was a sturdy vessel some 36 feet long, of 12 tons gross tonnage. She was built—or rather rebuilt—with this very object of ocean passages in view. In size and type she was the best that could be chosen for the job ; for that is the largest craft that one man's strength can reasonably handle alone.

*   *   *

The next great circumnavigation was that of Captain Voss : and it was made in direct emulation of Captain Slocum. Slocum's voyage was already famous : and a journalist, a Mr. Luxton, offered Voss a half-share in 5,000 dollars if they two could

sail round the world in something smaller than the
Spray. Captain Voss—who had amongst other
things been on a treasure-hunt to the Cocos Islands
—had considerable experience in handling small
craft ; and he was as fine a born seaman as Captain
Slocum (if not finer). But his choice of vessel was
far odder. He bought a fifty-year-old Red Indian
dug-out canoe in British Columbia—the builder's
skull being thrown into the bargain for luck.

This choice was not so crazy as it sounds. For
being carved from a single gigantic log of red
cedar, the *Tilikum* had no seams to open under
the pounding of the seas : she was all in one
piece.

She was 38 feet long, over all : but much of that
was a sort of dragon figurehead, which gave her
somewhat the appearance of a Viking ship. And
indeed her only considerable dimension was her
length : for even when finished and loaded her
draught was only a couple of feet. So she was in
fact much smaller than *Spray*. Voss strengthened
her with oaken ribs, and a keel and kelson. Then
he decked her over, and rigged her with three
small masts and four small fore-and-aft sails (for
easy handling).

Captain Voss had a rather more theoretical mind
than Captain Slocum (as his choice of hull and rig
suggests) ; and in particular he was interested in

the measure of safety which could be accorded to such small craft by the use of a drogue, or sea-anchor. Put simply, the theory of the thing is this. A vessel, driving before a heavy gale, even under bare poles, will move so fast through the water that the suction of her stern will seriously disturb its natural formation. The danger of this is that a following wave, rolling harmlessly over the surface of the sea, may be foundered by this suction and crash heavily on board. There is always far more danger to a small craft from getting " pooped " (from a wave coming in over the stern, that is to say) than from anything she may meet with her bows. Now Captain Voss believed, and afterwards demonstrated, that this risk could be reduced almost to *nil* by the skilful use of a " sea-anchor." This, in its usual form, is a canvas cone, towed over the stern as a sort of brake to reduce the vessel's speed when running, and over the bows to keep her head-to-wind when lying-to. Such sea-anchors were, of course, not in Voss's time anything new : but it was a spectacular demonstration of their usefulness when, with the aid of one, Captain Voss contrived to sail his dug-out round the whole globe ! And without doubt their common use to-day owes much to his practice and his preaching. But the safety they give is by no means automatic : and Captain Voss's success with them owed much to his extraordinarily skilful handling of them, and his unequalled knowledge of the structure and behaviour of waves.

Like Slocum, Captain Voss published a book on his voyages (*The Venturesome Voyages of Captain Voss*), which will never be forgotten so long as men sail. And, like Slocum, when it was all over he vanished at sea. Further, Voss (you will notice), like Slocum, was a professional seaman with many decades of practical experience. His craft was, in its own way, well chosen for its purpose. Unlike Slocum he was seldom entirely single-handed ; though few of his companions, understandably, lasted very long.

*   *   *

These two are the fathers of their art. Since their time they have been emulated in this way and that by many others : and it has now become a frequent thing for the Atlantic at least to be crossed by small, well-found yachts. Disasters are rare ; turning back, perhaps, is not so rare, for the strain of such a voyage on the crew is far greater than its strain on the boat. Most of the more recent crossings have been made by amateurs : crossings which throw an ironic light on the fuss in the papers when the *Endeavour* had, forsooth, to cross the Atlantic actually under her own sails (she was probably at least as safe, doing so, as the *Queen Mary*).

I will not attempt to list them : but will refer only to two of the best known of such voyages made since the War. Both were made by amateurs.

One of these was the Frenchman, M. Alain Gerbault. When he accomplished his East-to-West crossing of the Atlantic single-handed in the *Firecrest*, from Gibraltar to New York without any port of call, he carried out a great feat : for there is a world of difference between crossing the North Atlantic from West to East, and from East to West. For West to East the Atlantic is 3,000 miles wide : but from East to West it is at least 4,500.

This sounds like a riddle : but a glance at a windmap will give you the answer. The prevailing winds by the direct route are westerlies : and it would be tedious folly to attempt to beat the whole way against them. It is only by a large detour to the South, right into the Tropics, that the region of the North-East Trades gives a prospect of a fair wind even part of the way. And even that, it seems, cannot be relied on. *Spray* crossed, West to East, in 29 days : *Firecrest*, East-to-West, took 101. Three times as long.

Now M. Gerbault was not a professional seaman. He had been trained in his boyhood by Breton fishermen, it is true : but by profession he was a civil engineer. Nevertheless he had, without doubt, that natural physical aptitude which for want of a better phrase one might call " bodily genius " : that gift which all great seamen must have. But in him it had been shown first as a boy tennis-champion, then, during the War, as a pilot in the French Air Force. The *Firecrest* was slightly smaller than Captain Slocum's *Spray* : she was only 30 feet long : but she drew six feet to the *Tilikum's* two. She was wholly unlike either of them in build, for she was an old-fashioned English racing cutter of the deep and narrow type ; substantially built, but designed for racing rather than for an ocean voyage. In choosing her, Gerbault exemplified the modern theory that the best racing hull should be the best cruising hull also : the apparently greater comfort evident in something of the fishing-boat type being due rather to the latter's slower speed than to any really inherent virtue. All the same, it is plain that *Firecrest* knows how to roll !

* * *

Another and most remarkable amateur is Harry Pidgeon. Unlike Gerbault, he had never even seen the sea as a boy, but was a farmer born and bred : his sole nautical experience had been some adventurous canoeing on the Yukon River. But the worm of the wanderlust gnawed at him, and he decided to build his own ship from plans published in a magazine.

So the *Islander* came into being. She was a " hard-chine " boat : that is to say, a cross-section of her would show a corner where her side joined her bottom, instead of the usual round curve. This makes for comparative ease in construction : but hard-chine boats—even the famous Chesapeake Skipjacks—are never supposed to be so comfortable at sea as those planned with a kindly curve. Her construction, however, was immensely sturdy—so sturdy that when she afterwards was thumped by a gale for days and nights on a lee shore on the South African coast she took little damage. Her length was 34 feet.

It was during the War that Pidgeon laid down her keel ; and when she was launched he spent some time getting used to the handling of her, so it was not till November in 1921 that he set out from Los Angeles on his four-year voyage, via the South Seas and the Indian Ocean to South Africa, and home again by St. Helena, Trinidad (where he and Gerbault met, and visited each other's vessels) and the Panama Canal. Harry Pidgeon's book, too, *Around the World Single-Handed*, is one which may be read with profit.

These four voyages may be taken as four outstanding examples of their art. Now let me roughly summarize them. Each of these small vessels was between 30 and 40 feet in length, strong and well found, and of course decked over and provided with a good cabin. As for rig, they exemplified amongst them the three rigs most commonly used for small vessels (sloop, cutter and yawl): while the more uncommon three-masted rig of *Tilikum* recalls to mind the fast canoes one sees speeding over the Carribean. Again, of the men who sailed them, Slocum and Voss were professional seamen with a lifelong training; and though Gerbault and Pidgeon were amateurs, both had experience as yachtsmen before their great voyages were undertaken.

It will now be easier to estimate in comparison the extraordinary achievement of " Fred Rebell." *Elaine* was barely half the length, or a twentieth part of the tonnage, of those others : in fact she was a *boat*, whereas these others were all fundamentally ships in miniature. For alone amongst them she was not decked in. This means, of course, that one single heavy sea taken on board would send her straight to the bottom ; whereas the decked craft fears little that does not come in over the stern, and may survive even that—may even roll clean over and up again without sinking, as has sometimes happened. Again, consider the hardship entailed by that lack of any cabin. The only shelter was a canvas hood, such as road-menders use, through which the spray leaked continually. Except in fine weather nothing on board was ever dry : and at one time, when she had sprung a leak, Rebell's hands became so sodden with water that his fingernails began to come off. And he lived on board her, like that, for a year ! Yet he seems to have felt his hardships less than almost any other of these lone navigators— certainly less than M. Gerbault. But Gerbault is a civilized man : while Rebell seems rather to have the physical resistance and insensibility almost of an animal : and both in this and in his mysticism seems related to Algernon Blackwood's imaginary *Ur-mensch*, rather than to be one of the human race. Consider, moreover, that he was a farmer and carpenter, whose *sole* sea experience had been in the engine-room of steamers, and who apparently gave *no* preliminary time to learning the ropes before he put to sea ! Rebell himself attributes his success to Divine Intervention : and indeed, all things considered, it would be difficult for any but the most credulous to believe in any other explanation of it.

* * *

If his book were only a technical description of this extraordinary voyage, it would have an immediate and permanent interest for all yachtsmen and those interested in adventure ; yet would, perhaps, leave the general public cold. But it tells more than that. Such an extraordinary voyage could only be undertaken by an extraordinary man, moved by extraordinary motives.

" Fred Rebell " (his name and his passport, like everything else, were home-made) here tells you about that man with simplicity and frankness : his love-affairs and his visions of Almighty God, his progress from sceptic to Holy Roller. It is a record of a spiritual odyssey almost as remarkable as the physical one.

*   *   *

I do not know where Rebell is now, except that he is again somewhere in the South Seas. It was in December 1937 that I saw him, first and last, blown up on the beach at Aldeburgh in Suffolk. For as you will read in the final pages of this book, after he returned to Latvia the wanderlust attacked him again. So he bought a Baltic fishing-boat : and this time he decked her in. He also added a keel to her ; but being unable to afford the more usual materials of iron or lead, he adopted the somewhat unconventional expedient of building an outside keel of reinforced concrete. It had not the weight, of course, of iron : but it had the strength, for it stood grandly the pounding on a shingle beach of that on-shore gale which put him aground at Aldeburgh. It stood it so well that afterwards there was hardly a mark upon it ; and certainly no sign of it coming away from the hull.

In this new craft he intended to sail from the Baltic to the Pacific. But Fortune was not so kind to him as formerly. His first trouble, he told me, arose in the Kiel Canal, on the banks of which he had landed to help himself to a few potatoes. This seemed highly suspicious to the German officials, who arrested him and searched his boat : and found therein the manuscript of this book. The manuscript was in English : a damning circumstance, when the owner claimed to be a Latvian ! And it was a long time before they could be persuaded that the story you are about to read was meant to be literal truth : was not rather a code description of the most secret German fortifications.

His further troubles arose from the elements ; and they go to prove two facts, sometimes forgotten. First, that sailing in narrow seas is more dangerous than sailing in the ocean ; that it is land, not water, which usually wrecks a ship. Second, that amongst the world's narrow seas those round Great Britain rank among the most dangerous.

He had only intended to call, in these islands, at Plymouth (not because it is a good harbour, but because he hoped to make there the acquaintance of the Plymouth Brethren !). But a ferocious autumn easterly gale in the North Sea proved too much for even his endurance : and after two days and nights of it he was actually asleep when his boat was driven ashore.

There he remained, at Aldeburgh, all the winter ; making many friends locally, but forbidden by the immigration authorities to go to London even for a day. An impressive little man, with the imperturbably calm smile of the happy bigot. In the spring of last year he set out again : but again unsuccessfully. His unconventional keel might be well constructed, but it was not well designed : too long and straight for handiness : and after frightful experiences in the Bay of Biscay he was at last compelled to abandon the *Selga*. He did not, however, abandon his main project, but shipped in a little schooner for Australia, and from there made his way back to the South Sea Islands he loves. From them an occasional post card, dated from islands each remoter than the last, finds its way to England : welcome proof at least that Rebell has not yet dropped his hook, alongside Voss and Slocum, in the Port of Vanished Ships.

RICHARD HUGHES.

1939.

PART I

*

FRED REBELL IS BORN

Escape from Russia—A Second-hand Passport—" Fred Rebell " is Born—How to Treat Lunatics—Stowaway to Australia—A Settler on the Land

SURPRISINGLY little is needed to change the whole course of a man's life. A trifling incident, a word spoken, a book read, may jump him out of everyday routine, putting him off at a tangent, driving him round the world.

While I was still at college I read an anti-militarist novel by an Austrian countess (I forget its name, and hers). I was so stirred by the woes which that lady had undergone on account of war, that I said in my young mind, " No ! I will never take part in *that* lunacy ! "

* * *

I was born in Latvia. Latvia was then (before the Great War) under Russian rule. Military Service was compulsory. Pacifism working strongly in me, I decided I would not serve. So, when my time came for enlistment, I dodged the Frontier Guards, and crossed into Germany.

Liberty was a holy word for me : an intense passion : and I had fled from my homeland to find her. To Germany. The young fool ! She did not dwell in Germany. Imperial Germany was no " land of the free " : it was no better than Tsarist Russia, as I soon found out. For instance, no one could get employment there without showing his passport.

So I went to the Russian Consul : begged him for a passport with tears in my eyes. But he would not give it me : he said he could not give a passport to a deserter. But moved, apparently, by my distress, he directed me to a certain religious organization, saying they had helped many a young man in a position like mine.

But I did not go to them. I did not want charity : I wanted a passport.

Charitable organizations are supposed to supply the needy : surely that means supplying them with what they need. But they are limited in their ideas, and I have yet to learn of any charitable organization that hands out passports to those who need them.

While I was pondering over this difficulty I passed a shop where furniture and all sorts of household goods were being sold second-hand. It had plenty of custom : poor people who could not afford to buy things new thronged it. " Well," I thought, " if a second-hand bed is good enough, why not a second-hand passport ? " True, it would not be smart and shiny like a new one ; but a new one soon gets smudged and dirty from living in your pocket and being thumbed by greasy officials : and then, what is the difference ? True, it would be nicer to have a new one ; but if I could not get a new one, why be squeamish ?

In Hamburg in those days there was a public-house called the *Verbrechers Kneipe*, which means " criminals' pub." I soon found out that this was the chief Exchange of second-hand passports and documents of all kinds. Before long, I found there a passport which I could have at a bargain-price— only half a dollar. It was a bit grubby, but it appeared good enough to get me a job : so I bought it.

However, it turned out not such a good bargain as it looked. It was like this. I had decided on going to sea, so as to see something of the world— and perhaps even to find somewhere a country not under the Rule of Paper. But to go to sea, you needed as well as a passport a seafaring permit. So I went to the German Maritime Office to get one ; and, of course, showed them my passport, and claimed the name on it. Had I been to sea before ? they asked me. " No." So then the official started looking in a great ledger.

5

" What ! " he said. " What do you mean by saying you have never been to sea, and right here are entries for three different voyages on three different ships ? "

So now I saw why that passport had been so cheap ! " Paul Sproge " (the man I was now) must have been a seaman, and have deserted his ship somewhere, so losing his seaman's book (which, of course, the Captain keeps until you are discharged). No wonder he had been so willing to sell his name and his passport, seeing all they were really good for was to get one into gaol !

" I lost the book," I said.

" Then don't come here telling lies," shouted the official, " or I will fetch the police."

Well, I thought, as I walked out, that is just too bad. But after all this is a good passport : it only wants a minor adjustment. It only wants a new name on it. You don't throw away your watch because one of the hands is bent, you fix a new hand. So I went to a chemist and bought some stuff, and soon the old name was gone.

That was the end of " Paul Sproge." When a young applicant for a seaman's book next appeared at the Maritime Office, the name on his passport was Fred Rebell. " Fred Rebell " could not have three ships registered against him, because he had only been born half an hour before. The

youngest seaman in all Hamburg. They gave
" Fred Rebell " the seafaring permit all right, and
it was not long before he got a job.

You think I did wrong ? What wrong had I
done ? Papers do not mean anything, anyway. A
man means something, and work means something.
If a government is so crazy that it will not let a man
have work unless he has got papers, then it is
only rational to humour that crazy government like
you humour any other sort of lunatic. Suppose you
were sitting in a room and a crazy man jumped in
at the window. " Are you Julius Caesar ? " he
says. " If you are not I will kill you."—" Certainly I am Julius Caesar," you would answer,
edging for the door. And would your conscience
worry you for that ? Well, I was in the same
position—up against something crazy that was
stronger than I. " Certainly," I said, " I am Fred
Rebell. It must be so, because it is written on my
passport."

—Reader, you do not often get a moral at the
beginning of a story : but I am going to give you
one now. (Maybe there are other morals, but I
will save them for later.) All those big militarist
countries with their emperors and their thrones
and their armies and their guns and their frontiers
and their frontier-guards and their officials, and
above all their passports : see them on one side,

and see me on the other, a young idealist student who had run away from home and lived with the lowest of the low. I ask you, which would you say was the stronger if you had seen us then? Which looked as if it would last the longer? And yet, where are those empires to-day? Under the sod. And where am I? Here, and not only a living man, but to-day a happy man—which is a lot more than I was then.

—But back to my story. Fred Rebell became a seaman, and began to find his way about the maritime cities of Europe. In Antwerp in those days I found hundreds of conscientious young men who like myself had deserted their militarist countries and, in the endeavour to find liberty, were mingling here with sailors and with the scum of the earth. To meet their need of passports just the ordinary second-hand trade would not have been enough. Here was a mass need, which only mass production could satisfy. An underworld factory was working here at full blast, and a set of faked papers (technically called " rags ") of almost any country could be obtained for a few dollars.

Seafaring, however, is not a bed of roses. My parents had given me a college education, and I lacked both the strength and the endurance necessary for the occupation I now engaged in. Once when I was trimming coal in a bunker on a German

8

mail-boat the engineer came in and remarked, " You have a nice easy job here." How stupid that remark sounded to me ! How lacking in insight the man must be, not to guess how heavy the wheelbarrow felt in my hands, how sore and stiff was my back ! Easy ? Why, I had never worked so hard in all my life. But come what might I never looked back ; and with the incessant demands put upon them, my strength and endurance rose within a year to the required level. The engineer was right : I began to find that the work after all was easy—comparatively speaking. I even acquired enough proficiency for promotion, and qualified as a stoker.

It may be that the soul of a man is the whole true man : but if so, the body is a tool in the soul's hands. Just as a good workman cannot do much without a good tool, so the soul is better for having a well-forged body to work with. That is what my body had now become : a tough, hardened tool, accurate and reliable. And so I have kept it.

But even during that time of hardship there were compensations now and again. I would catch glimpses of strange lands, would take a stroll on a foreign shore, see other cities and places. However, before long these attractions faded, strange places began to look the same : I wanted to settle down, and I wanted to pick from the whole world the right country to settle in. For some time it was passportless England that attracted me ; and then later it was sunny Australia I set my heart on.

That was in 1907.

Yes, but getting to Australia would not be easy. The fare alone cost sixteen pounds. I had saved that much : but if I spent it on the fare I would be penniless again when I landed. Now I ask you, what does a Rational Man do with his money ? He buys something with it : something to eat, something to wear, something to plough with—something at any rate he can hold in his hand and keep. But if a man spends his money on a steamship-fare, what has he bought ? Nothing. All he has done is get himself moved from one place to another—after which the money is gone. So I decided it would not be rational of me if I spent any money on going to Australia. I ought rather to travel there free.

That is what I did (after first mailing my money, addressed to myself poste restante, Sydney). I stowed away. Knowing the ropes I stowed away well, where I could not be found. It turned out I was by no means the only would-be Rational Man on that ship : there were fifteen other stowaways found—and put ashore before she even left Gravesend !

After she had been three hours at sea, yet another stowaway turned up. He was not discovered : he thought it was safe now, so he came out of his hiding-place, and wandered all over the ship looking for somebody to report to. At last he went right up on to the Captain's bridge, to report to the Captain. The Captain resented at first what he thought was a passenger's intrusion on forbidden ground. But when he realized it was merely a stowaway anxious to report himself he said with a smirk, " You are just in time, my friend ; the pilot will be leaving in half an hour and you shall go with him ! "

But *I* knew the sounds of a ship, and lay hidden till several hours later, when I knew by the stopping of the engines that the pilot was being put in his boat. Half an hour after that I made my appearance, and reported to the Chief Engineer. At first he would not believe I had stowed away—at any rate, not under the stokehold floor. I looked too clean. I had to show him the suit of clothes I had been wearing on top of the other ones before he would believe me. So they nicknamed me King Neptune on the ship, and found work for me in the coal-bunkers.

At Sydney General Post Office I collected the money I had remitted myself from London, and said good-bye to seafaring.

11

After a few months' wandering about the country, I settled down in West Australia, on one of those bits of land which the Government was giving away free to settlers. Free ? It was dear at the price, being covered with a tangled growth of forest. I cleared a small patch of what looked like good ground, and sowed it with a few beds of vegetables. I watered them whenever necessary : but they did no good. Especially the peas : the most any one plant produced was one pod with one pea in it ; and some of them did not even do that. So when I harvested my crop what did I get ? About half my seed. The other things were much the same. And all the little forest birds and animals ! A little speckled bird, no bigger than a man's thumb, used to come round now and again tugging at the newly sprouted turnip-seedlings till he had them up by the roots, when they quickly disappeared down his throat. How I wished he would wait till they were big enough to choke him !

Many men in those days gave up farming at this disillusioned stage ; but the endurance I had won at sea would not let me. I saw the forest was the trouble : you could not grow things right under its petticoat, so to speak : it must be pushed right back. And then the land would need money put into it before it was any good. But I had no

12

A West Australian feller chopping off a Kari treetop

money to put into my ground. So I saw I had somehow to get some. Meanwhile, I concentrated on clearing the timber, and thus qualified at a new job—handling an axe, and dealing with timber of all sorts.

Luckily, there was a sawmill in the locality ; and wages were high in Australia in those days. Here was a chance to make the money I needed ! So when I was not cutting my own timber I was cutting timber for the sawmill. I spent two years like this, and saved five hundred pounds working at the sawmill—all of which I put into my land. That way I got a farm at last which would grow something.

CHAPTER II

Wanted, a Wife—Lonie—The Great War—A Friendless Girl—Marriage—Paulie—The Amorous Engine-driver— I become a Carpenter—A Divorce—A New Love

WHEN I had my selection shipshape, the next thing of course was getting married. That did not look too easy in the West Australian Bush, because one thing was lacking there—girls. Nor would it be much use looking for one in the towns, since town girls had not much appetite for sharing the hardships of a settler's life.

Having been very busy these last years I had not kept up a correspondence with any of my boyhood fancies ; but still, I could remember the names of some of the girls who had been at school with me, and I wrote round them to see if one of them would marry me. Presently I found one who said she was willing ; so I sent her steam-boat fare over to her.

Then I started in getting the place right for her. But judge of my disappointment when I got a cable from Colombo, saying, " Sorry not coming : must return."

14

That was all I heard from her, from then on ; but it seems she left the boat in a hurry, and forgot a package of letters, and these one of the stewards handed over to me on arrival. Among them was one from another lover, in Latvia, begging her to return : and since he was willing to pay her fare back, just as I had paid her fare out, there had been not so much to choose between us on that score : and she chose him.

Well, that was no good.

But by now I had ceased being put off a project by small checks. So I decided to advertise in the Latvian papers—that a lonely young settler in Australia wished to correspond with young ladies : view, matrimony. The response was most gratifying. I received over thirty letters (with photographs) from ladies willing to take the risk. Some were ugly (possibly with hearts of gold) : others were passable, and two were distinctly pretty. Of these two, one was a cultured young lady, a school teacher by profession : so she would have made a suitable mate for me. But as I thought the Australian Bush and hardships of pioneer life would hardly be the right environment for her, I ruled her out.

The other one was a country girl, by the name of Lonie ; aged twenty ; an orphan, living and working on the farm of her stepmother. Her case appealed to my sympathy (and also I argued that it would not give her much cause for home-sickness).

I did not, this time, send her the whole money for her fare : thinking I was being prudent, I just sent her enough for her to get to London, and arranged for her steamship ticket to be waiting for her there.

But those militarist countries had not done with me yet ! They had one more chance to have a crack at me. This was 1914, and meanwhile the World War had broken out.

Lonie could not get direct to London : so she took a train for Archangel—not exactly the right direction for Australia, perhaps, but it seemed better than staying in Latvia with the German armies advancing. Then presently I got a letter from her, saying that she had taken a passage in a schooner from Archangel to England. The schooner was not going to London, and she asked me to send her ticket and instructions to the port where she was landing.

This letter nearly drove me frantic, because of course it took nearly three months to reach me—a fact which apparently did not enter her head—and she would have been in England long before that. Alone in England, I pictured, was now this girl who had consented to be my wife. Stranded and

friendless, unwanted, without the language of the
country, vainly trying to reach me, not knowing
that a steamship ticket for Australia waited for her
in London !

And well might I worry !—but of that more
anon.

So, judge of my surprise and delight when
presently I received a telegram that Lonie was
actually in Australia ! For I had almost given up
hope of ever seeing her. I hastened to meet her.
But alas ! That meeting was Dead Sea Fruit.

I might have guessed what would happen to a
friendless girl, cast among mariners. The Captain
of the schooner had paid attention to her, she said,
on the trip from Archangel : at first she refused
to listen to him, but presently part at least of her
heart, it seemed, was lost to him.

The sad tale was soon told. Thus it was with
very mixed feelings that this young couple about
to wed met each other on the docks at Fremantle.

I was undecided in my mind what I ought to
do. Should I send her home again ? Honour demanded it. But what home, with war raging over
Latvia, was there now to send her to ? So I said,
" We will make the best of it. I am responsible
for bringing you here, and henceforth I will take
care of you. Maybe that we will learn to care for
each other." So we were married shortly after

17

at the Registrar's Office. For Lonie, alas, like myself at that time, was a sceptic, and did not hold with church ceremonies.

When eventually a boy came into the world, there was not that gladness or rejoicing that there might have been had we learnt to love each other as we had hoped.

We called the boy Paulie—he grew into a bright little lad. But as I looked at the baby, I could not help longing for the day when there should be one born of our true mutual love.

Then a strange and tragic thing happened. Three days after her confinement, Lonie got out of bed, while I happened to be away ; went into the field, and dug some potatoes. Swinging half a sackful of them on to her back, she did herself an injury, so that never again could she bear another child. Whether this was wholly an accident, or whether it was in some way due to the sadness attending the birth of her first-born, I cannot say.

Nevertheless, after about a year we really did become very fond of each other. But it seemed almost as if a curse had fallen upon me. The sad beginning of my marriage was only the first of those misfortunes which now fell on me, each worse than the last. A young heifer broke its back, a draught-horse fell in a swamp-hole, the cattle became afflicted with rickets : and to crown all, our expensive pedigree sow died of sunstroke.

So, in order to keep the three of us, I was compelled to give up farming for the time being, and to go back to my former work at the sawmill.

If this had not happened I have little doubt that Lonie would have remained a loving wife to me : if I had remained always with her, that is to say. But while I was at the sawmill she was lonely, and became acquainted with an engine-driver—a good-looking young man, and obliging.

But it was not so much his looks, it was his manner of handling the big locomotive that did the trick with Lonie. Every day as it passed our farm he would open up the throttle till, rolling and snorting like some giant monster, the locomotive would rush madly along the single track—a performance which soon had her quite madly head-over-ears in love with him (but I still feel it is an unfair advantage to make a publicly-owned locomotive serve your ends in love-making).

From now on, Lonie became most unhappy. It is surprising how dense some people can be, times without number. Not suspecting the cause of her unhappiness, I blamed the farm set-backs for it. I blamed the isolation, and life on a farm. This will not do, I thought ; I cannot have Lonie as unhappy as this.

19

So, seven years after our marriage, I sold the farm and took her to town—first to Fremantle, and then to Perth, where I got a job with a large contracting firm as carpenter (considering that I had never learned the trade but was just handy with tools I was lucky in this).

But Lonie's reaction to town life should have shown me what was wrong with her. She went to shows, dances, parties and whatever attractions the city offered : but she seemed unhappier than ever.

Still unsuspecting, I thought maybe I was not giving her comfort enough : our home was too bare and ordinary. I could not give her luxury on a carpenter's wage, so I began scheming out some way of making money quickly. I thought of a plan for building wooden cottages for workmen by mass production ; and all my spare time and evenings I spent in planning, drawing, and making specifications. I even floated a small company to make a sample house. I told Lonie about my plans, because I thought if she saw any chance of our rising in the world that might give her hope. But she took no interest. Sometimes even she would rail at me over trivial matters.

One day, exasperated at this railing, I cried out at her, " If I am not good enough for you, you had better find someone else who is."

To my surprise she seized on that as if she had been waiting for it. " Yes," she said, " you find someone you care for, and I some one *I* fancy. That will be far better than living a life of misery ! "

So, in the twelfth year of our marriage, our home was broken up. We were not divorced— not then.

That came later. Lonie sent Paulie to me with a message that she had decided for her freedom.

So the case came on : and as I read it in the papers I nearly laughed. What a curious dish one's own intimate affairs make, garnished with a sauce of legal language, and served up for public consumption ! What a monster, all unbeknown to myself, it seems I was ! Even that fatal sackload of potatoes was mentioned—but as a task which I had cruelly set her!

I do not like to remember or record all the details of those sad days. I said I nearly laughed when I read all this nonsense in the papers : but there were two special reasons why I should not do so. The first was that I discovered Lonie had forgotten altogether a promise about alimony : and I found myself let in to pay her an almost impossible amount. The second reason was that a new star was appearing in my life—Elaine. For her alone I now lived. But as yet she had given me very little encouragement. What sort of help would it be to a suitor if the lady of his heart read that sort of stuff about him in her evening paper? Read, and believed it?

CHAPTER III

Elaine—Her Beauty and Her Shortcomings—True Love at Last—Rejection—A Broken Heart—Damp-proofing

DRIVEN by discord at home, and by the need to take my mind off business worries, I had lately acquired the habit of going to public dances twice weekly. It was there I had met Elaine—just a demure, dark-eyed, dark-haired Australian maiden of nineteen summers.

Soon I knew all about her. She was to be seen any day in a busy general shop on a corner of Bedford Street, dexterously serving the numerous customers. Often I would stand in the doorway, worshipping my goddess from afar. I admired the black of her hair, the lustre of her dark, crystal-clear eyes, her nicely arched eye-brows, her slightly convex Australian nose, her finely delineated lips. I thought her my perfect counterpart ; my long-sought-for missing half, without which I should never be complete. Love like this had never come to me before. I liked the way she dressed, her maiden modesty, her quick intellect, her courteous manner, her low and clear voice ; and I loved to hear her speak my name.

Defects and blemishes ? Did she have any ? I should say so, for who is there without them ? First, she had protruding knee-caps. But what are protruding knee-caps when a man loves as I loved ? I loved her for her charms, and had nothing but compassion and apologies for her shortcomings. If those knee-caps were slightly more prominent than goes with a shapely leg, was it not a shame that she had perhaps been compelled to scrub floors or do other housework that should cause them to be so ? Or had she come by them in some even more meritorious way ? Was she, perhaps, a Roman Catholic ; and had acquired them by too much praying ? However she had come by them, they were undoubtedly to her credit !——And if Elaine's teeth were somewhat blackened and decayed, I only felt indignant and sorry that she had been compelled to grow up on an unhealthy, unsuitable diet.

Elaine, too, had freckles. The casual stranger would never have guessed it ; but a close look betrayed them under the coat of face-cream and powder on her face. But what was that to me ? Immediately I fell in love with her freckles, and came to hate the coating of powder which concealed them. Yes, I loved her just as she was : and had I seen any other faults in her, either physical or temperamental, I should have loved her just the same.

Whenever I went to dances, my eyes would scan the hall for her presence : and dancing with her of course I counted a treat.

Once I even went so far as to see her home from the shop.

But I was too slow and reserved in my attentions. I did not then suspect to what flame the initial spark in me would grow. Not till it was too late. For there came one evening at the dance when I received a shock. *My young lady had chosen another beau !* There on the verandah sat the two of them, taking no part in the dances, her head reclining against his shoulder.

My blood boiled.

There was no more dancing for me that night. I went home and penned her a letter in which I told her I would have given a fortune to be in the other fellow's shoes that night. I besought her not to throw her affections on him in a hurry, and to give me at least one interview.

Next day I took the letter to the shop ; bought some trifle of her, and then said, " I have written you a letter : would you care to read it ? Will you reply ? "

" Yes, I will answer it."

I left it with her. But no reply came, nor did I ever see her again at the dances. Evidently her young man was taking her elsewhere.

25

How was I able to bear the anguish which the next weeks meant for me ? Hope dies slowly, and in me particularly so. When no answer came to my letter I sent her another : but that, too, evoked no reply. Then I went once more to the shop and besought her for an interview. " If you have anything to say to me," she answered, " say it here."

" I need more privacy than this shop can afford," was all I could think of to reply. But her heart seemed stone.

All this time, while passion for her was burning me up inwardly, I was falling away outwardly. I came to look wan and aged, and could hardly take any woman's fancy. Pity, perhaps ; but not fancy ! One lunch hour, as I was sitting by the roadside near to where I was working, thinking of Elaine, an elderly lady approached me, and handing me a paper bag said, " Excuse me, please, but by the look of you I think you are unemployed and starving. There are some hot meat-pies in the bag."

I felt staggered. " Thank you, dear lady," I said, " but I am neither unemployed nor starving : my trouble is of the heart, not of the stomach, and I don't think you can help me in any way."

The irony of it ! Business had never been better. I had given up the building scheme : but now, in company with a partner, I had gone in for another branch of the building trade—damp-proofing. Our business boomed in Perth, and presently my partner went to Sydney to establish a branch there also.

Other men might have sought solace from the pangs of love in dissipation, but not I. I sought it in my work ; and the more hollow worldly success became for me, the more it came to me almost unsought.

But this sort of thing cannot go on for ever. I felt at last that I must leave Perth. But I must see her once more before leaving. So one day, after tarrying a couple of blocks away in indecision, I drove up in my Ford to the shop. I had at last a premonition that my suit would prove entirely hopeless. She saw me coming, but kept dressing the shop-window, with her back towards me. " Elaine," I said, " I want to speak to you."

" What do you want ? " she replied crossly, turning on me.

" I will be leaving the State shortly, and I wanted to see you before I left. I long more for the sight of you than I do for the light of day. Whatever have I done to you, Elaine, that you should treat me in such a manner ? "

" I do not wish to be bothered by you," she answered, returning to her work.

These words of hers, heavy with tragedy, sealed my fate. I realized at last that there could be no more argument about it. Somehow or other I staggered out of the shop ; managed to crank up my Ford and drove away.

I opened the throttle. If it had done forty, fifty, one thousand miles an hour, it would have been none too fast for me.

But the old Ford could not travel at that rate.

CHAPTER IV

*The Great Depression—On the Dole—Thoughts of Suicide—
A New Plan—My Boast to the Consul—I Buy a Boat—The
Elaine Described—Fitting Out—I Make a Sextant—My
" Chronometers "—I Make a Taffrail Log—Study Seaman-
ship—Draw my Charts—Passport Trouble—Again a Matter
of Conscience*

NOT long after, the world-depression hit Sydney
(whither I had removed). One of the first trades
to suffer was the building trade. The architects
who used to give me work soon found difficulty
even in keeping roofs on their own houses. Other
trades followed. Soon there were thousands of
workers clamouring to the Government to give
them bread ; and had the Government not introduced the dole, surely there would have been
revolution. For five months I was without work,
and my savings dwindled. During that time, what
was it gave me fortitude ? It was the thought of
Elaine.

Wherein had she found me deficient ? In
courage ? Manliness ? I would acquire them. If
at the swimming-bath I trembled before some
particularly high dive, I had only to say to myself,

" *Elaine* would have me do it ! "—after which I
flung myself into the air as boldly as a bird.   Education, then ?   I spent whole evenings at the public
library, even sometimes trying to write in the style
of the authors I read there (without that training,
perhaps this book could never have been !).

But the time came when my savings were
exhausted, and the only hope that I had was to
get into the queue at the Relief Department.   So
for the four following weeks I carried home Government milk, meat, sugar, jam, butter, tea and soap.
These were four terrible weeks.   I had reached
the very bottom of dejection, my measure of dis-
illusionment was about full, and life seemed entirely
worthless.   " My God," I cried, " whatever have I
done that this should come on me ?   I lose the
affection of my wife, I am scorned by the one I
love dearer than self, and now—I am living on
the dole ! "

There seemed only one way out, for me : the
way which many were taking every day in those
times : the leap from the Gap (the cliffs at the
mouth of Sydney Harbour).   This was a higher
dive than any which I had forced myself to take
hitherto for Elaine's sake !   This would be the end
of one born so obviously a misfit in life.   But
even as I stood there about to take the plunge, a
notion crossed my mind.   My sufferings were, after

all, mental. A mariner does not scuttle his ship to rid it of infesting rats, nor the farmer cut down the cherry-tree to spite the marauding sparrows. What use was it for me to destroy my body, when it was my soul that was tortured ? If there be no Hereafter, well and good : but was there none ? *For sure ?* If there was one, I had better learn something about it before I went there. So I retraced my steps from the Gap, and returning to the Public Library read all the books on the Hereafter I could get hold of.

Meanwhile, however, another scheme formed in my head. Might I not emigrate to America ?

I called on the American Consul. But he gave me little encouragement. He told me of the immigration laws, how difficult it was to get a permit to stay there. Only a small number of immigrants were being admitted yearly ; and of those, almost all were relations of people already living there. I should have to remain for years on the waiting-list, he told me, for a visa.

How this scene recalled an earlier one, when I had asked the Russian Consul in Hamburg for a passport ! How weak I had seemed then, and how strong the Russian Empire ! Yet where was the latter now ?—Was I one, then, to be intimidated by the lack of certain little marks on paper ?

Looking the Consul in the face, I told him something that I knew would surprise him. " In a short while," I said, " I shall be in the States. I shall not pay my passage there, nor stow away, nor work my passage as a seaman. Moreover I shall stay there as long as I like ; and when I want to I shall leave ; and I shall ask no visa from you or any other Consul."

As I left, the Consul looked at me as if I was a lunatic.

But I was not speaking at random—my plans were already made. . . .

However, whatever I had said to the Consul, I could not fly to America like a bird. My plan would need a *little* cash, at least. And the only way to get cash was by work.

But how to get work ?—— Work, I reasoned, is always to be had if one values one's services low enough. And so it proved. I got a job as handyman at thirty shillings a week—hardly one-fifth of what I had been earning at the best. From this followed a similar under-paid job as carpenter, building sea-side cottages. But low though the wages were, I managed to save the small sum that I needed.

*　　　*　　　*

For twenty pounds, I bought a second-hand eighteen-foot C.B. sloop, of the type that has been perfected for racing in the sheltered waters of Sydney Harbour. She was not decked in, of course; and I could not afford to deck her. Her draught was only eighteen inches and her free-board twenty inches.

In that boat I intended to sail to America. Was ever an ocean voyage projected in a more unsuitable craft?

Built for speed and lightness, it was plain that her hull would never stand the battering of big seas. So I strengthened it, by doubling the number of her ribs and by fixing an outside keel. As for shelter, the best I could contrive was a canvas hood amidships (which would at least keep the spray off me). And I enlarged my sail.

But buying and improving the boat was not the only expense entailed. This voyage might take me a year, and I had to provision her. True, I could replenish my stores at islands on the way: so I provisioned her with only six months' supply of dry food. I packed it all in paraffin cans, fitted with screw caps: plenty of flour, that is to say; rice, wheat, pearl-barley, peas, beans, sugar, semolina, rolled oats, and powdered skim milk. Also dried fruit, potatoes, onions, lime-juice, olive oil, treacle, and yeast. I also took on board thirty gallons of water, in tins and drums which I had lined with asphalt (and it kept remarkably well like that). But because I was provisioning her at the minimum cost, I could allow myself no luxuries. I took no tinned food ; no tea, tobacco, spirits, or medicines.

My rationing allowed for one and a half pounds of dried food per day, and about one-third of a gallon of water. I might, of course, hope to catch some fresh fish ; and sea-water would have to serve me instead of salt.

For cooking purposes I shipped a Primus stove, a bottle of methylated, matches, and five gallons of paraffin. I also stowed on board an electric pocket-torch, my kit of carpenter's tools, paint, pitch, bits of wood, nails, and all sorts of odds and ends that I thought would come in useful on the way. The total cargo weighed, probably, half a ton.

But there are other things a mariner needs, besides a ship and food and water. He needs navigating-instruments, and charts. And these are expensive—far beyond the means of a man as hard-up as I was.

By the airs the makers of nautical instruments give themselves, you would think no one could do their work who had not been serving an apprentice-ship of one hundred years ! Well, I would have a try.

The most important instrument of all, of course, was the sextant, since it is with that you learn

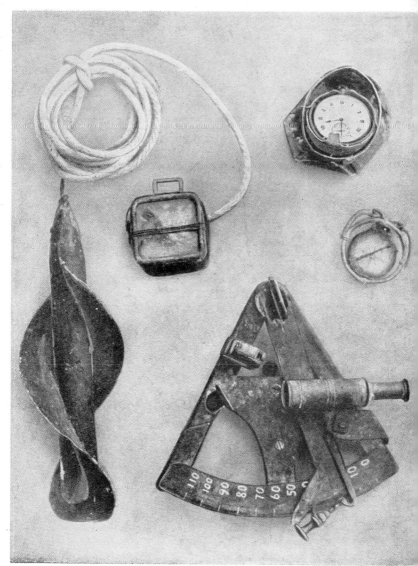

Home-made navigating instruments

your position (when out of sight of land) from the
sun and stars. It has to be extremely accurately
made because the slightest fault in it may cause
your computed position to be wrong by hundreds
of miles. Well, the materials I used for my sextant
were several pieces of hoop-iron ; a Boy Scout
telescope (price one shilling) ; an old hacksaw-
blade ; and a stainless steel table-knife.

I broke pieces off the table-knife, to make the
mirrors. They had to be ground optically flat,
which I accomplished by melting a lump of bitumen
on to them for finger-grips, and by rubbing them
over emery-cloth laid on a piece of plate-glass. I
used three grades of emery-cloth—coarse, medium
and fine—and finally I gave the steel a mirror
finish by rubbing it on a damp cloth with red oxide
(or jeweller's rouge).

The hacksaw-blade, of course, was for the degree-
scale. I chose it because of its regularly cut teeth,
and because I could bend it into an arc. I so chose
the radius of the arc that two teeth made one
degree. I took the temper out of the blade so
that I should be able to reshape the teeth, and for a
tangent screw I took an ordinary wood-screw that
would engage nicely with the hacksaw. This way,
I could read half-degrees of arc straight off the
teeth of the hacksaw. But half a degree of latitude
represents thirty nautical miles, and you need far

35

greater accuracy than that. So I enlarged the head of the screw, and sub-divided its circumference by sixty. Thus I was able to read to minutes of arc off the screw-head itself (each minute corresponds to *one* nautical mile only).

That was the hardest job to make.

The next thing I needed was a chronometer. Well, I could not make a chronometer ; but I bought two cheap watches (each as a check on the other) for a few shillings. I slung them in gimbals, so that the motion of the boat should not affect them.

Next came the taffrail-log ; which is the instrument that records how far you have travelled through the water since it was last set. A spinner is trailed in the water, and that turns cogs which actuate a dial on board. I made my spinner from a bit of broom-stick, to which I set aluminium blades at such an angle that the spinner would turn once for every twelve inches of passage through the water. For the indicator I adapted a little clock, gearing it down so that every minute on its face should mean one mile of distance sailed. When I tried this log out, I found there was a slip of twenty per cent. : but an error in a nautical instrument does not matter, provided it is constant and you know it. You can allow for it. And until the time when the works of the little clock corroded

The author taking a sight
Trying out the boat in harbour

with the sea air and water, this taffrail-log served me well.

But what did I know of sailing ? And what of the arts of navigation ? Precisely nothing. Seamanship I read up in Sydney Public Library ; and I practised handling my boat a few times in Sydney harbour. As for navigation, I bought a seventy-year-old manual of that art and put it on board : time enough to study it when I was at sea. Charts too were things I could not afford to buy ; so I copied them from a somewhat ancient atlas in Sydney Public Library. It was not till later that I found the disadvantage of having used it, as some of the islands I came to had not been discovered when that atlas was drawn.

There was still something lacking. A ship, even more than a man, in this world, needs " papers." I ought to have a bill of health, a passport, and all sorts of other useless rubbish.

But once again there were reasons why my conscience prevented me from asking for a passport. While *I* had been working and saving on my minute wage, Sydney had been full of loafers ; men and women who preferred to do nothing and live on the dole, rather than to sell their services for what they considered too low a price. It was bankrupting the Government—as I soon found, when I came to change my remaining cash into dollars, and found how the Australian exchange had fallen.

Now, just about that time I received a demand for arrears of taxes. If I paid those taxes, I should be encouraging the Government to waste the hard earnings of thrifty men on the lazy and improvident. This my conscience would not let me do. However, unless I paid my taxes I could have no passport.

There was only one thing for it, then—to slip out to sea quietly, with no papers at all.

PART II

*

THE VOYAGE

(Sydney, December 31st, 1931, to Los Angeles, January 8th, 1933)

CHAPTER V

*Departure from Sydney—A " Buster "—The Two School-
boys—Seasickness—" Good-bye, Australia ! "—Elaine Sails
Herself—I Jettison My Mandolin—Dirty Weather in the
Tasman Sea—An Improvised Sea-anchor—A Leak—A
Novel Leak-alarm—I Mend the Leak—Longitude Com-
putation—Four Weeks at Sea—I Miss New Zealand—I
Mend a Watch*

FOXY BRIAN and his gang—friends of mine—were
on the jetty to see me off.

" You are in for a big contract," said Foxy.   " If
you find the going too hard, come right back."

" Thanks," said I, " but I am not returning
from this trip.   Whatever I meet I will face it."

" Too bad, too bad ! " said old Foxy, sadly.
" Well, our best wishes go with you : and don't
forget to write us when you get there."

" O.K."

I cast off, and with the faintest of breezes made
my way slowly down the harbour.   It was nearly
noon, and for the last time I checked my sextant
by the meridian altitude of the sun.   It proved to
be fairly accurate ;   my calculated position only

differed by two or three miles from my known position.

Shortly after, I passed under the great harbour bridge. It was now nearly completed. Would I ever see it again, I wondered?

Had I taken any notice of evil omens, probably I should never have gone outside the Heads. For, beating down the harbour, I carried on too long on the inshore tack, and bumped a rock! First evil omen! Second, a mile or two farther down I got caught in a " buster." These " busters " are sudden squalls, and common on hot afternoons. Had I kept my eye on the shore-line I might have seen it coming, in a swirl of dust. But I was not keeping a proper look-out ; and before I knew what was happening, the " buster " was on me. The sail flapped wildly, and the boat heeled over till water was pouring in over the gunwale. Then away she tore with the boom scoring the water— until I was able to get the mainsail down.

Within a few minutes the placid waters of Sydney Harbour had been whipped up into quite formidable waves. Should I run for shelter till it was over, or should I keep on?

Just then I caught sight of a little sailing dinghy, right out in the middle of the harbour, manned by two schoolboys. She was tearing along under full sail, bouncing on the waves like a kangaroo. " If those two kids have courage to carry on, so ought you," I said to myself, " in your bigger boat. If you have to run for shelter before you are even out of Sydney Harbour, what will you do if you meet a storm in the open ocean ? "

So under jib alone I sailed out through the Heads. Outside there was a big swell ; but my boat rode it nicely. I rode it less nicely, however : I was seasick. But that attack of seasickness only lasted half an hour ; and since then I have never been seasick in my life again.

For a long while I watched the receding shore, and as dusk was approaching I stood up in the stern : waved my hand towards the land, and sang out, " Good-bye, Australia ! Good-bye, sweetheart ! Good-bye for ever."

*   *   *

Presently the stars appeared. I felt tired with the day's exertions. So I lashed the tiller, and turned in to sleep—while the southerly wind bore me ever farther from the country which had been my home for the last twenty-five years.

I had about six hours' sleep that night.

Next morning the wind had moderated. I set the mainsail, headed her due east, and carried on comfortably at three or four knots.

—People often wonder how a man sailing single-

43

handed manages to steer at night. The answer is
very simple. The wind steers for him : not only
at night, but nearly all the time. Indeed, I doubt
if during the whole of my voyage I spent more
than an hour a week actually at the helm. You
can balance a boat to sail at almost any angle to
the wind (except dead into it, of course) which
you may determine. This you do by the set of
the sails ; tightening in this sheet, slackening out
that one, putting in reefs or shaking them out till
you get the balance you want. For the final minor
adjustments you lash the tiller an inch or two
to port or starboard. So long as the wind stays
steady, you will keep on the same course this way ;
but if the wind changes, either in direction or
force, the job has to be done again if you are to
keep the same course by the compass. However,
out in the open ocean the winds blow steadily for
quite a long time. At night I used to wake up
once or twice, flash my torch on the compass to
reassure myself, and then turn over to get some
more sleep. It only happened a few times in the
whole voyage that on waking I found myself going
in a totally wrong direction.

If you are in narrow seas, of course, there is
danger in this method, since an unexpected change
of the wind might carry you well off your course
and run you ashore. Or if you are navigating by

dead-reckoning only, you would be liable to lose yourself ; since you would have no record of how your boat had travelled while you slept. But the tactics of the ocean sailor, with no dangers to bump into, are not so much concerned with keeping an accurate course as with getting ahead, at the best speed possible, in a direction as nearly the right one as will suit the existing wind. A point or so to port or starboard is no great odds. For the ocean sailor is not dependent on dead-reckoning to tell him his position. He determines that from time to time (whenever the weather suits) with his sextant.

*   *   *

I had made the preparations for my voyage with considerable care ; but of course I could not anticipate every little trouble that might crop up. Spray splashed on my canvas hood, for instance ; and I soon found it was not so waterproof as I had hoped. In fact, everything under it got saturated. Three days out I discovered my mandolin was so soaked with water that it had fallen to pieces—and I had to throw it over the side. My bedding and blankets also were soaking wet, and sleeping in them became a nightmare. It was nearly a week before a day came fine enough to enable me to dry the bedding a little, and to put another coat of waterproof dressing on the hood.

Indeed, fine days were the exception at this the beginning of my voyage. The Tasman Sea has a bad reputation for storms : and though this was supposed to be the good season, I did not altogether escape them : and general bad weather seemed to be the rule.

The day would begin bright and sunny ; but soon it would cloud over. The wind would grow in force till it began to howl in the rigging. Sails had then to be reefed and double-reefed—or perhaps to come in altogether. The swell would rise, until it swept along in tremendous waves in whose valleys a house or a ship would be hidden entirely from sight.

Then the crests would form white caps or breakers, which rushed along with a roaring noise, and tossed the boat as if it were a chip.

Many a time at the height of a gale have I stood by the mast, and watched the breakers come ! Here, with the speed of a racehorse, is an angry header approaching. It looks certain that the boat must be swamped or engulfed. But no. She rises to meet the sea : there is a slight impact : the spray flies up : the boat shivers in every joint, and is tossed perhaps eight or ten feet to one side or the other—but the breaker has passed under, and with foam and roaring, vanishes in the wake astern.

I felt sorry for the little boat, for the battering

46

she had to stand. But she rode the seas bravely, and never shipped a wave green. And indeed, contrary to popular belief, the motion of a little boat, particularly if under sail, is not nearly so bad as you would imagine. The up-and-down movement cannot be felt at all ; for there is none of that heave one experiences on big ships.

As confidence in my craft's sea-worthiness grew, something of the Viking spirit stirred in my breast. No matter how rough the sea, I felt content so long as my boat was forging ahead. The seagulls and the fishes will bear me witness, that often in a gale I would break out into a wild and reckless chant.

On the other hand, if I were becalmed or my boat making no headway, I felt miserable.

Only one gale gave me really serious concern. I had taken down all sail and was drifting broadside on to the breakers, occasionally taking a good bucketful of water on board. At any moment she might ship one green, and fill. So I set about rigging a drogue, or " sea-anchor." I tied two oars crosswise, and stretched a piece of canvas on them till the thing resembled a kite. Then I weighted one edge so that it should ride upright in the water, and flew—or rather, swam—my kite on a long rope from the boat's bows.

The purpose of course of the device was for it

to act as a drag in the water, and keep my bows into the wind. For half an hour it did this very effectively : the boat rode with her nose into the breakers, and took never a splash on board. But alas, this did not continue for long. The rope of the sea-anchor chafed on the bobstay, and parted ; with the result that I lost both sea-anchor and rope as well.

Once more she swung round broadside to the seas. There was only one thing to be done. I hoisted my smallest jib, and ran before it.

These actions sound simple and easy, described ; but they were not carried out without discomfort— to put it mildly. I had no oilskins to wear, and only my canvas hood to shelter under. Whenever I had to be outside in bad weather I got drenched. Once, when all my clothes were wet, I had stripped and rolled myself in blankets. Then a sudden squall made it imperative to lower the mainsail. I dashed out naked. That squall was a hail-squall, and during the next few minutes my bare back received such a father and mother of a hiding as I did not remember since my young days.

As time went on, and bad weather continued, the head-winds and constant buffeting began to tell on my boat. Presently she developed a leak in the bows, down near the keel. The leak got steadily worse. I tried to caulk it from inside ; but the sea

48

kept pushing the caulking out. Presently water was coming in so fast that I had to bail the boat every two hours. That was all very well by day ; but not so easy at night, with no alarm-clock. So at night I laid an empty paraffin can in the bottom of the boat. As the water rose the can would float, and then begin to bang merrily against the sides. I had to trust to that noise to wake me up in time to bail.

It worked all right, as an alarm-clock. But all the same the thing began to get on my nerves. Besides, my finger-nails were nearly soaked off by continual wetting.

So the next fine day that came along, I lowered the sails, and went over the side with a handful of soft pitch. This I rubbed well into the crack under water ; and to my great satisfaction the operation proved effective.

Luckily there were no sharks about : but my need was so desperate that I should have attempted the job even if there had been.

*   *   *

My course lay due east : and as I progressed eastward, the sun would rise and set earlier day by day. Likewise, of course, noon would come round sooner ; so that on my fourth week out from Sydney it fell at 10 a.m. (by Sydney time). Now every four minutes of difference in time corresponds to one degree of longitude : so I knew that I was now thirty degrees of longitude east of Sydney.

This method of longitude computation is simple in principle : but it is not always so easy to carry out as it would appear. For in order to ascertain exactly the time at which the local noon occurs, two observations are needed : one in the morning, and one in the afternoon. The sun's altitude at the time of the first observation is recorded ; then a second observation is taken, to discover at what time the sun has sunk to exactly this altitude once more (noon, of course, will be the mid-point between these two times). But suppose that when the time comes for the second observation, the sky is cloudy ? All chance of ascertaining your position that day has gone. And during these weeks the sky was so often cloudy that I determined to master other methods, requiring more calculation but more often practicable. By the use of tables and logarithms I learned to compute my longitude with only a single easterly or westerly observation of sun, moon or planets. For latitude, however, I still relied on the highest or noon altitude of the sun.

I had intended to call at Auckland in New Zealand : but after four weeks at sea I found I was already far to the east of it. I had missed New Zealand altogether, having been driven a couple of hundred miles to the north of my intended course. So it would now be easier and safer, I realized, to make for the Fiji Islands at once, rather than to try to struggle back south and west again. So I abandoned all thought of New Zealand, and changed my course to due north.

I had been on the ocean now for fully four weeks, without sight of ship or land. But indications began to appear showing that islands could not be far away. A milky tinge had crept into the steel-grey of the ocean, blending it a greenish colour ; from which I concluded that the sea-bottom had risen to less than a thousand feet from the surface. I also saw quantities of seaweed floating about : and there were more birds.

Without doubt I was in the neighbourhood of the Kermadec Islands. But unfortunately those were some of the islands which, as I have mentioned, were not included in my chart ; so I could not tell just how far from them I was.

As I continued on my northward course, the gales soon moderated to steady south-easterly Trades, and sailing at last became a pleasant thing. For nearly a week the boat kept so truly on her course that I had no need to touch either sail or tiller. It was now, with little to do, that I began to feel the lack of company. And yet I cannot say that I was bored. The ever-billowing ocean, the sea-birds and the fishes were enough to hold my attention.

Also I read, wrote, and studied. I found that solid reading—books of study, and Longfellow's poetry—suited me well ; but I could arouse no interest in fiction, or frivolous stuff.

I also got into the habit of expressing my thoughts aloud. For instance, on getting up in the morning, I might say to myself, " We will have some breakfast now "—and then proceed to carry the idea into action.

Cooking took up some of my time. I did it all on the Primus, and even in the roughest weather managed to get the stove going at least once a day—if only to boil a kettleful of cocoa. In the finer weather I even made bread on it. I would ferment the dough, and then steam it in a tin over the stove. It would be very much like bakers' bread ; only a lot heavier, and without a crust. Or, for a change, I would fry some fritters, or make a johnny-cake. For breakfast, I had porridge with treacle or milk. For dinner, I had wholemeal bread and oil, with hot cocoa. For tea, if I were lucky enough to catch any fish, I had fish-and-chips.

I no longer now feared disasters : but I had my share of minor nuisances. I was surprised, one day, to notice a film of paraffin on top of the bilge-water. I found that my paraffin can had rusted through, and about half its contents had leaked out into the bilge. Moreover, it had spread everywhere, and had softened the bitumen coating of my food-containers. So for a week I could handle none of them without getting my hands dirty.

Moreover, I had to be particularly careful with fire, or my boat would have gone up in smoke.

My watches, too, began to give me some trouble now. The salt water had got into one of them, and it had stopped some time previously. Now the other one failed, the hook breaking off the main-spring.

I am not a watchmaker ; but it was a necessity to me to get this watch going again, as my navigation depended upon it. Somehow, with the boat pitching, I *had* to fix a new hook on to the main-spring, and get the watch going again more or less accurately. In doing this an earlier experience stood me in good stead. Once before, in Sydney, I had tried my hand at a similar job. Exasperated at the rascally ways of watchmakers, I had determined to carry out my own repairs, and fit a new main-spring myself. I had learned the art at the same school as I learned seamanship (i.e. by skimming through a book on watchmaking at the Public Library !), and had then successfully fitted a new spring. Thus, I was now not altogether without practice, and managed to carry out the repair successfully.

As I was travelling north, and knew before the watch stopped on what meridian I was travelling, I had only to set the watch by the sun to have the correct time once more.

CHAPTER VI

MY boat was pressing steadily northwards, and soon I found myself in the Tropics.

The steady Trades now gave way to changeable winds : to overcast skies, rain, thunderstorms, and a steamy atmosphere. Visibility became poor, and even in daytime I could see barely a couple of miles ahead.

I knew that I must be getting near the Fiji Islands : but as I had not been able to get a noon sight of the sun for several days, I did not know *how* close I might be to them. At night particularly I felt there was a serious risk of running on a reef in the dark.

It is all very well having a sextant, and the art of navigation at your finger-tips : but if the sky is overcast day after day, and no sight can be had of the celestial bodies, how are you to tell where you are ? You are as lost as a child in a dark room.

It was in this extremity that I thought I would try prayer.

Bowditch on Navigation makes no mention of prayer as a means of finding one's position at sea. He relies entirely upon navigational instruments and sights of the sun : he never tells you what to do when such sights cannot be obtained.

Up till now I had been, as the reader will have realized, a sceptic. For twenty-five years I had never said a prayer. Ever since my student days, I had prided myself on having that rational mind then fashionable among the intelligentsia ; and all my life I had been guided by it. But looking back over my life, I could not see that it had guided me very well : neither into great achievement, nor pleasant courses. Indeed, few lives can have been so disastrous and futile as mine had hitherto been.

Again, you will remember how it was reflexion upon the possible duality of man—the existence side by side of soul and body—which had held me back from suicide that day at the Gap, and had wakened in me the glimmerings of interest in that unknown part of me ? Now, separated by so many hundreds of miles of water from the life I had lived, alone with Nature, and left in the lurch by the achievements of rationalism, was it to be wondered at that I turned again to consider my soul ? And from my soul, to consider the God

Who made it, and the possibility of appealing to that God for help ?

So about an hour before noon I said the following prayer :

"*God Almighty, Who hearest every prayer, please let me see the sun at noon, so that I can take a sight.*"

Would my prayer be answered, I mused ?   Since I had got into trouble through my own fault, the Almighty would most likely let me get out of it the best way I could.

Does God still take an interest in human beings and love them (as the Bible says), or has He brought them into existence and then forgotten them—left them to battle alone against the forces of Nature ?

While I mused thus, I reflected also upon the difficulty of the thing I had asked.   The sun was hidden not by a single, but by a double bank of clouds.   If God should deign to answer my prayer, He would have to make at the right time corresponding gaps in *both* these banks, on a line joining the sun to my boat.   There was little room for Chance, if such a thing should happen.

I was still reflecting upon this rather sadly, when I noticed the hood of my boat brighten.   " Hallo," I said to myself : " the sun is going to appear after all !   It is not yet noon ; but I will take a sight all the same, since at noon it will probably have gone again."

Sure enough, the sun appeared shortly, nice and clear. I took out my sextant, obtained a good sight, and then went to my watch to check the time.

It was twelve o'clock exactly, by ship's mean time!

A couple of minutes later the sun was already dimming, and by twelve-five had disappeared for the rest of the day.

This gave me food for thought. If it was a coincidence, it was a most remarkable one indeed. If on the other hand it was an answer to prayer, there must exist some power, some kind of energy unknown to science and unmeasurable by the scientist's most intricate instruments, yet invocable by simple prayer.

Perhaps, after all, the billions of people who have prayed in the past, the millions who are praying to-day, have not entirely deluded themselves, as the sceptics and atheists would have us believe.

*   *   *

The sight I had obtained disclosed that I was still one hundred and fifty-five miles from the southernmost Fijian island shown on my chart.

The weather continued unsettled and muggy on the next day, too : and though I had made good no more than thirty miles to the north, I awoke on the morning of the second day (8th February, that was) with the firm conviction that land was in sight. I came out to look. The sun had just risen in all its golden glory, and as I scanned the horizon I did see land, about ten miles to port. Yes, there was no mistaking it : those two little brownish-green mounds, sticking out of the ocean, were undoubtedly land. I nearly shouted for joy.

Forty days I had been now on the waves, tossing in a little boat, putting up with all sorts of inconveniences and discomforts. So the prospect of a change, of a day ashore, of some fresh fruit, some rest, was welcome indeed. Besides, the sight of land reassured me that I was not entirely lost on what had seemed for so long to be endless ocean.

On approaching them I made out two fair-sized islands with smaller ones between. The wind died away in the afternoon, so it was near sunset before I got close to the land.

A submerged, brown-looking reef, which the ocean swell was breaking in great rollers, encircled these islands : and beyond the reef there was a narrow stretch of emerald green water, calm as a pond—the lagoon. But I could see no entrance to this lagoon : and as dusk was approaching, I decided for safety's sake to put out to sea again, and return in the morning.

So till midnight I sailed southward ; and after midnight, back again towards the north, thinking in that way to return to the spot I had left by sunrise.

But the breeze must have freshened in the night ; for it was only two o'clock in the morning when I was wakened by a strange noise like the breaking of surf on a sea-shore. I jumped out of my bunk : peered into the murky darkness, wondering what it was. A low black cloud seemed to hang over the horizon, and below it there seemed to be a strip of clear sky from which the noise, now fast growing louder, emanated.

With a sudden start I realized that this was no black cloud but solid land ! That apparent strip of clear sky was the foam of breakers on a reef ! My boat seemed to be gliding through air ; and looking over the side I could see wondrous phosphorescent gardens and coral growths, rising from the deep and with their fronded paws reaching ever closer to the keel of my boat. The heavy swell from behind lifted me, and passing under curled into a roller : then—barely a chain in front—precipitated itself noisily into a seething sheet of phosphorescent foam all over the reef.

If I wanted to save the boat I had not a moment to lose. Quickly I threw over the tiller : and luckily for me, the boat responded well. But I had several anxious moments as I watched my boat breast the next on-coming roller almost at the point where it would break.

I did not get much more sleep that night : but dawn found me sailing along the reef.

The biggest of these islands proved to be about a mile long. Vegetation was sparse, and there was no sign of human dwelling. Some of the smaller islets were mere rocks, that had been undermined by the surf until they resembled cabbage-heads—or mushrooms resting on short, stumpy stalks. Northward, as if growing out of water, could be seen the heads of palm-trees.

I felt disappointed, and began to give up any idea of landing. Had there been any sign of life, or had I known what a battle I should have before I reached Suva, I would have landed here at all costs, and rested till the weather changed. But instead, I decided to push on : to Suva, the capital of the Fiji Islands.

Before I left them I took the latitude of these islands by a noon sight of the sun. When I worked it out, I rubbed my eyes. There must be a big blunder somewhere. For they were more than one hundred and twenty miles south of the southernmost islands marked on my chart !

That was on the assumption, of course, that I was correct in my longitude : that it was the

Fiji group which was concerned. But was it possible, I wondered, that my watch had gained fourteen minutes during that forty days at sea, and that in consequence I was on the longitude not of the Fiji, but of the Tonga Islands? Some of these, I knew, lay as far south as this. But if that was the case, I was seven hundred and fifty miles to the east of where I thought I was! And, what was worse, I had no chart of the Tonga group. Consequently, I could neither identify the islands I now saw, nor find my way through the group—if that in truth was where I was. In that case my position would be most hazardous, and it was impossible to tell when (if ever) I might reach Suva.

Nor could I keep sailing the ocean much longer: for my supply of drinking-water was getting low, and my running rigging was badly worn—the rope so full of knots and splices that it hardly looked like rope at all. To cap it all, the wind was dead against me.

With all these cares on my mind, I fell asleep: but barely had I dozed off when I heard a kindly but authoritative male voice say distinctly in English close to my ear, " Trust your instruments ! There are islands in the Fiji group farther south than those shown on your chart."

It startled me. I woke, jumped out of the

bunk : looked round, thinking that someone had come aboard. But my eyes beheld nothing but the murky blackness of night, and the tumbled ocean around me.

What voice could that have been, I wondered ?

Anyhow I had little option but to trust it, and to sail on for where I believed Suva to be (and indeed, when I reached Suva I learned that the voice had been a true one : for there *were* islands to the south of the Fiji group not marked in that old atlas from which my charts were copied).

So I faced now resolutely the head-winds, which seemed to conspire to make my progress as difficult as possible. For some unknown reason the boat no longer seemed to sail so well : after four days' battling, which by dead-reckoning should have brought me one hundred and sixty miles to wind-ward, I found by the sun that I had only made good ninety miles. I was making quite abnormal leeway, for some reason.

Even worse weather, however, was in store.

I was treated one evening to a wonderful spectacle : against a background of streaky cirrus clouds the sky was filled with towering cumulus, and every colour in the rainbow could be seen in that sky in the most gorgeous blending. Lucky Fijians, I thought, to gaze at such marvellous skies ! But in truth this was no ordinary sky, even for the Fijians.

It was (as I might have guessed) the precursor of a storm.

It blew hard the next day, and the swell that rose tossed my boat as it had never been tossed before. Part of the day I could hoist no canvas at all. Towards evening she would just bear the jib : but the weather continued squally and unsettled for a couple of days more.

According to my reckoning, and if the Voice had spoken truly, I had now approached within eighty miles of the main island—Viti Levu. As this island rises four thousand feet above sea-level, I ought to be able to see its peaks in the morning, if the weather were clear.

But the clouds and steamy air gave no prospect of clearing.

I was eager to know as soon as possible whether my navigation was right : whether a known course lay ahead of me, or disappearance into an unknown ocean : and I decided to try prayer once more.

" God Almighty," I said, " should the peaks of Fiji be within seeing distance, please let me see them at sunrise to-morrow."

Next morning, as the sky coloured, I was up on the forepeak, scanning the horizon. Visibility was bad : banks of cloud and mist everywhere, no land to be seen. Either the land was not there, or *this* prayer was to be unanswered.

Suddenly a sharp breeze sprang up on the starboard quarter ; sending my boat along at a smart pace, and throwing the spray up in showers. " Too wet to be on deck," I said to myself ; and vanished under the hood.

But after a little while it occurred to me that the strong breeze might have cleared away the mists. So I took another peep ; and sure enough, far ahead, about half a degree above the horizon, there loomed a darkish-grey shape resembling the hip-roof of a house.

Was it land, or cloud ? At so great a distance as this—perhaps forty miles—they are hard to distinguish from each other. If cloud, it would change its shape ; so I waited for half an hour ; but no, it remained unaltered.

Then the sun rose, and not long after the sight was blotted out. Not till late in the afternoon, when I had drawn some twenty miles closer to it, and the sky had once more cleared, did I catch sight of this mountain again.

This time there was no mistaking that it really was land ; the summit of Fiji's highest peak, projecting above the clouds that surrounded its base.

I felt happy. My navigation had been sound : the Voice had proved credible : and two prayers had been answered.

65

CHAPTER VII

I Land for the First Time—The Rocking Earth—The Chinese Schooner—Natives—The Bar of Nature—Native Cooking—I Join the Dance—The Market—The Fire-Walkers of Mbengga.

PERHAPS under the influence of land, the weather now changed. I had only forty miles to go to reach Suva : but I was making very slow progress. Other islands dotted my course : where there are islands there are reefs, and night-sailing in consequence became extremely dangerous. I began to feel the lack of sleep. I had also broken into my very last gallon of drinking-water. So presently, when I drew near a small island covered with luxuriant vegetation, I decided to call there.

I sailed round under its lee, dropped my hook, and then—so as to be able to work in to shallow water—hauled up the centre-board.

I thought it might be a bit of a job, hauling this up after it had been down for so long ; but to my surprise it came up more lightly than usual. I soon discovered why. Only the top of it was still there ! All the bottom part, which should have

66

projected below the keel and acted as a fin, had carried away. So that was why my boat had sailed so badly the last few weeks! Why it had slipped so many miles to leeward, and been ready to heel over in the lightest of breezes! Disgusted, I chucked the remaining remnant of the board into the sea.

Then I waded ashore, and found myself at last on solid ground.

But, solid ground? This was not solid ground! It rocked and heaved under me like a raft. With every surge of surf on the beach the whole island seemed to heave and tilt under me, so that I could barely keep my balance, and staggered like a drunken man.

Reason told me it was myself that must be afflicted in this way, and not the island. And indeed this was the case: after two months in a tossing boat I had lost my shore-legs entirely.

It was only by adopting a swaggering sailor's gait that I presently was able to get along at all.

I began to explore, traversing the shore for half a mile each way. There was no sign of human habitation anywhere, nor even of animal life. Tall coconut-trees fringed the island: and behind that fringe were gullies where a profusion of shrub, tree and creeper crowded each on one another, blotting

67

D

out the blue of the sky. Amongst them I noticed pawpaw-trees and bananas with bunches of unripe fruit. A sombre shade hung over this grove, and a smell of decaying vegetation permeated the air. And a silence. Nothing stirred : a lizard scurrying out of my way, a hermit crab withdrawing into its shell, were the only bustle and tumult that the island knew.

Moreover, I found no stream, nor any sign of drinking-water. So I picked up a few coconuts that were lying on the ground, and returned to my boat. I decided to sail round to the windward side of the island and look for a settlement. But that must wait till to-morrow : night was closing in, and the first thing was to find a safe anchorage for a proper night's rest.

I lifted my eyes towards the setting sun : and a strange sight met them. About a mile away, and as far to right and left as the eye could see, the whole horizon—just above the blue of the sea—appeared to be studded with a row of pebbles, boulders, and pillars : with here and there among them a white line of ocean rollers breaking into foam. It was the outer reef surrounding the island, now laid bare by the receding tide. How I had got inside it, I knew not : by sheer good fortune the flood tide must have carried me through some passage or over some low-lying part of it.

The Chinese Schooner

As I stared at this reef my eye was caught by a sail—the first I had seen since I left Australia. It grew larger : and presently through a gap in the reef a small schooner appeared, brought-to in the lagoon, and anchored. I pushed off my boat and sailed towards them ; for here evidently were people who knew the place, and who could give me useful information.

She turned out to be a Chinese fishing and trading schooner of forty tons. Her crew numbered only two : and you will guess that it was only with the greatest difficulty that I was able to make myself understood by them. But when they gathered that I had come from Australia they became very interested, and indeed cordial. They had just finished their meal, but they offered me some cooked rice and tea, which I gladly accepted ; and they pointed out to me a safe anchorage for the night.

What a relief it was, after all I had gone through, to be swinging gently at anchor all through the night ! No worry about getting off one's course, or of running into a reef !

Next morning, when the rising sun lit the island, it looked from my quiet anchorage as pretty as a gem. If only I found water, I could be happy there for a week at least, I felt : there would be so many things of interest to me. So, after break-

69

fast, I waded ashore to explore further—the first
need of all being water.

Presently I came on a little stream trickling
down a valley. But the water in it was quite
brackish, and unusable. Then I found a road, that
seemed to lead right across the island : so part
at least of the island was inhabited. I followed
this track until I came in sight of some native
huts, and heard the laughter of children and the
barking of dogs. Where there are huts, I argued,
there must be water. So my anxiety on that
point was set at rest. But for the moment I must
return to the boat : for in a strange place I did
not dare leave her long unattended. Moreover, I
discovered that her bottom was thickly covered with
a growth of weeds and barnacles—another good
reason for my lack of progress recently : so I drew
her into shallow water, and set about scraping her
clean.

It was while I was busy on this job that some
natives suddenly appeared on the shore. Savage
cannibals ? Not a bit of it : one glance dispelled
every doubt. The men had a certain dignity
and reserve about them which inspired confidence
and respect—albeit they were coffee-coloured, and
garbed in loin-cloth only.

There were also some women with the party,
dressed in the long sarong or loin-cloth which reached

to the ankles. They showed less reserve than the men, gazing both at myself and my boat in open-eyed surprise—and if I looked at them their faces would spread in broad grins, their demeanour would be coquettish and they would try to draw me into conversation. But alas! I could but shake my head, and reply, "No savvy." There were children, too: lively little things: some without a stitch of clothing—scattered along the beach frolicking and searching for land-crabs.

Presently one of the men climbed a palm-tree and knocked down some green coconuts. With large knives they chopped holes in them and drank the contents: then they offered me one. It was the first drinking-coconut I had ever tried, and I found the quart of juice within it a very tasty and refreshing drink. Lucky islanders! Here at the Bar of Nature all comers are served free of charge.

One of the men could speak a little English, and asked me if I had any matches. I gave him a box, and he seemed delighted with it; for it seems that most of the natives smoke, and as they have not enough money to buy matches they have to carry fire with them, or else produce it by the laborious process of rubbing wood against wood. Imagine the tedium of that, you smokers with your matches and your petrol-lighters!

When I explained that I needed drinking-water, they told me that there was none to be had on this side of the island : I should have to get it at the tank at the village on the other side. So I weighed anchor, and sailed round. The whole village of about two hundred souls turned out to watch me land. When I had anchored, a canoe came out to take me ashore. Then they all crowded round me, to shake hands, to ask me where I came from, what I came for, where I intended going.

Then the head man, who was also missionary and teacher, invited me to his house for a "kaikai" or meal. His was the largest and most pretentious hut in the village. From outside it looked (like the rest) no more than a haystack with a door-opening in it : but inside it was nicely finished, and had a wooden floor whereon a large mat was spread. The meal was served in the middle of the mat, and six of us men sat round it.

I expected the food to be crude : raw fish, perhaps, and green coconuts. But I got a surprise ; for the variety of the dishes and the manner of cooking would have done credit to many a European table. We had baked fish, steamed breadfruit and taro, stewed giant clam in curry sauce ; and a delicious salad of pawpaws, tomatoes and bananas.

All this the natives eat with their fingers : but they gave *me* a knife and fork.

When the meal had been cleared away, kava (the native drink) was served in coconut bowls. It tasted to me like cold unsweetened coffee. After that, some of the ladies came in and sat in a circle round the room. Then I was offered a chair, and invited to watch a dance which was to be given in my honour.

For orchestra they had a boy beating a wooden drum : and as soon as he began, all present burst out into a chant which they accompanied with clapping of their hands. Then two young women stood up, locked hands, and started to hop together round the room. When they got in front of me they curtsied, and invited me to join in. So thus invited, nothing loath, you might have seen (had you been there) Fred Rebell, that plaything of a tragic fate, that melancholy philosopher, footing it lightly round the hut with a dusky lady under each arm, in a sort of Fijian turkey-trot ! It was years since I had laughed out loud : but now I could not help bursting into wild bellows of laughter : I laughed till my cheek-muscles ached from this exertion to which they had been so long unaccustomed.

After this first dance, two more matronly ladies gave me a turn. I was beginning to dance, now, with real spirit : but somehow I did not enjoy these two partners as much as the former ones ; for by the smell of them I could tell that they badly needed baths.

The dancing over, the ladies discreetly withdrew, and my hosts spread mats on the floor, inviting me to lie down for a nap—all Fijians usually sleep after a meal. But I can never sleep in the daytime : so I went for a stroll through the village. I counted about thirty huts scattered in the shadow of coconut palms, and there was also a stone-built school-house or church. Then I discovered the large concrete tank, half-full of rainwater, on which life on this island was wholly dependent. For the ground water there was all too brackish to be usable.

It did not appear to me that these people did much work. Except for a few fowls, pigs, and dogs, I could see no animals here. There was perhaps an acre planted with taro : but that, with the exception of a patch or two of flower garden near the huts, was the only ground that appeared to be cultivated. Probably fish is the staple of their diet : for when presently a native called me into his hut, many fishing spears were hung on the walls.

Presently I went down to the beach. Here the two Chinamen whom I had met the night before had spread various wares on the ground, and were doing trade with the natives ; and I stayed to watch. It was an odd sort of market : no money passed : all the transactions were recorded in a book. Some system of barter, I supposed. In addition to the Chinamen, there was a native banana-buyer, chaffering. Other natives brought him large bunches of bananas from a distance, and the buyer was very busy packing them into crates. His schooner would come for them in the morning, he told me : and take them to Suva, where they were worth about a halfpenny a pound. He spoke good English, and gave me other information too. The name of this island, he said, was Yanutha ; the distance from Suva was thirty-five miles : and once you got past Mbengga (the island next to this one) there were no reefs in the way.

So, to replenish my stores, I bought bananas and mummy-apples (papayas), and filled two cans with water at the tank. Then I took one more stroll round the island, and early the next morning set sail for Suva.

But those thirty-five miles took a lot of making. Near Mbengga the wind failed completely, and it looked as if I should never get away from that island. It was mountainous : and I was often to find later that mountainous islands play havoc with the regular breezes : you should steer as far clear of them as possible. Especially is this necessary when you are dependent on the steady direction of the breeze to keep your boat from sailing into danger. This I nearly found to my cost the following night, when I woke up to find my boat in the breakers near a submerged reef a few miles east of Mbengga. It was a flat calm, and luckily my boat did not bump. But I had to use the oars to get to sea again out of the breakers.

I did not land on Mbengga, though I might have done so with profit, seeing it is the home of the Fijian fire-walkers, who walk barefoot over a bed of red-hot stones. Devil-men they are called by the natives. The ceremony is only performed on festal occasions. I believe the practice hails from India.

It seems strange that these people never raise a blister nor scorch a hair on their legs during these uncanny performances.

CHAPTER VIII

Arrival at Suva—Three-headed Cerberus—The Fiji Times—
*Fame : Her Pros and Cons—A Merry Picnic—A Be-
witching Maiden—Fijian Economy—The Stranglehold of
Tariffs—The Straits of a Chieftain—" Malua " Fever—I
Learn My Punishment—April* 20th : *to Sea Again*

IT was not till the next day that I came within
sight of Suva. Outside the reef, my position certain, I took a sight of the sun to check my time-
pieces. When I had made my computation I was
astounded by the fact that within a second or two
I still possessed the right time—so close was the
computed longitude to the one shown by the chart.

It seemed nothing short of miraculous that in
spite of two months' run, and in spite of the tem-
porary stoppage and the changes of temperature,
my cheap watch should still be showing the right
time. The mysterious Voice which had told me
to trust my instruments had certainly spoken no
vain words !

I had no proper chart of Suva Harbour, and so I
missed the entrance channel, and had to work my
way through the reef past two little islands to the
east. At last, however, I sailed up the harbour,

tied up my boat at a good place just past the wharf, and went ashore.

I had a letter of introduction to a certain Mr. Osborn in the Harbour Master's office, and so I called on him first. He thereupon rang up the doctor, the police, and the Customs, to get me through the formalities.

The doctor came first. He wanted to know how I got there : where I came from : whether I had a Bill of Health from Sydney : whether I knew that I was liable to a heavy fine for coming ashore without first hoisting the quarantine flag : whether there was not infantile paralysis in Sydney : whether I knew the regulations : whether I had a supply of medicines on board, and whether I was myself in good health. I *was* in good health—I was even still in good health after the strain of answering these questions. The Police Chief came next. He was a tall Englishman, suspicious and aloof : he did not even shake hands before getting to business. For every question the doctor asked, he asked three : and it was fairly plain he did not believe my answers. To the policeman I suppose no one but a desperate escaped criminal would travel in such a way as I was travelling. No one would trust himself to the mercy of the sea like that unless a noose at least would be his portion if he remained on land.

Nor was my lack of a passport likely to reassure him. I told him that I held it sufficient for a man to possess body and soul without a paper label tied to them : but plain though the logic of that appeared to me, it did not seem to impress *him*. And when he asked me how much money I carried with me, he was again rendered suspicious by my refusal to tell him. On his part, he said that the regulations required him to know : but on my part, I deemed it prudent to keep the secret to myself : for the doctor had threatened me with a heavy (but unspecified) fine : and for all I knew the fine would be fixed at exactly whatever sum I proved to have with me !

However, at last the policeman was satisfied that what I said was true, and that I was no fleeing convict ; and after him the queries of the customs officer were small—a flea-bite. I had nothing to declare, and told him so. Thus at last this three-headed Cerberus of officialdom was appeased, and I was allowed to wander out into the town a free man.

I had not gone far, however, before I was accosted by the editor of the *Fiji Times* ; and he, of course, started to question me all over again. His questions, however, were politely put, and were answered on my part with far greater freedom and goodwill than I had answered the official enquiries. Thus it was that for the first time my voyage was made known to the world at large in the columns of the public press. Fame came to me over-night : by the morning everybody in Suva knew about me. I had sprung into prominence all of a sudden, and I had to face it. I disliked seeing a lot of people permanently gathered round the place where my boat was tied, and hated being stared at in the streets as if I was an elephant : it worried me having to answer the same questions over and over again. But on the other hand, such publicity does have its pleasant side. It brought me invitations to the homes of countless new friends : it brought me offers of help of every conceivable kind. Nor could I help being flattered by the more intangible aspects of glory. My boat was named *Elaine*, of course, after the Star of my Life—and there are a number of little girls running about the streets of Suva to-day who are called by that name, being christened during my visit ! Moreover, I learnt later that my voyage had even proved an inspiration to a poetess in far New Zealand. I will not quote her ode, for it is very long ; but the title of it read

"The Little Gay Homme in the Vest"
(*with humble apologies to the composer*
of the real song : "The little Grey
Home in the West").

And it repeated in verse everything she had read in the newspapers about me.

*   *   *

My first Sunday in Suva, a motor-launch containing a party of English chugged up to my boat, and I was invited to join them. They were going on a picnic. So I gladly crowded in amongst them.

First we went to the reef, which had just been laid bare by the receding tide, and there spent an hour or two looking for pretty shells and for " cats'-eyes "—those peculiar round pebbles which a certain mollusc grows to close the entrance of his shell. Had I known the price those " cats'-eyes " were fetching in America, I should have loaded my ship with them.

Then we went to a small and lovely island in the harbour, where we lunched : and then off again once more, up a river. We passed native villages, and abandoned plantations, till at last we came to a secluded bathing-nook. Here we put on bathing-suits, and plunged in.

Now, while we had been looking for cats'-eyes on the reef, scattered about in small groups, I had attached myself particularly to a sweet young lady of seventeen : a dark blonde with sky-blue eyes and fine features—a snow-lily, transplanted into the sunny south. Now whilst we frolicked in the shallows, I suddenly saw her eyes light up, and before I knew what was happening she had sprung at me. Her arms went round my neck, her legs round my waist ; and a bewitching smile played on her face, as if challenging " Now what will you do ? "

Above all things in the world I would have liked to kiss her ; but with all the company watching I dared not. I only muttered stupidly, " I will duck you."

I made an attempt, by leaning over. She dodged it. I took a step towards deeper water—and then in a moment we both were under. She had to let go then, and swim to safety ; but not before both of us had swallowed some water.

Once she was in the shallows I shouted to her, " Now you will not do that again ! "

" Won't I ? " she answered.

I could not help admitting that this young lady had a lot of charm about her. Could it be possible, I wondered, that there are really other fish in the sea, and that my heart is capable of loving someone else besides Elaine ?

It was a fortnight before I saw Sweet Seventeen again ; but one evening I was taking a stroll on the Parade, and there on a seat I saw her, with a few others who had taken part in that picnic.

I strolled over, and one of the ladies said, " We

are having an argument here : some of us claim that you are a hero, whilst others think that you are mad : what do you think of yourself ? "

" I think I am half-way between the two," I replied. " In other words, just a plain fool."

" Oh no, you are a hero ! " emphatically burst out a little girl of twelve, " and I have always wished to meet you."

" But, Loma," said one of the ladies, " what is the good of your meeting Mr. Rebell ? What can you do to help him—except perhaps pray for him ? "

" Yes," replied Loma, " I will pray for him."

" That is very nice of you," I said : " and as long as you are praying for me I am sure the ocean holds no dangers for me." And from what I heard later Loma kept her promise. Who knows but that it may be owing to her prayers that I am living to-day ?

Indeed, the man whose broken heart could not be healed by the sympathy and friendship of the fine people I met in Suva must have had that organ run over by a steam-roller.

Fiji is a rich country with an abundant rainfall and a warm climate. Everything grows there in profusion, and the land could easily support ten times the population that is on it now. But the native Fijian, though a stalwart muscular great fellow, good-natured and intelligent into the bargain, has one failing—he is indolent and easy-going, and dislikes applying his energies to a task for any length of time. " Mataka " (" to-morrow ") is his answer to the prospect of any unpleasant task. Wild Nature has supplied him for many generations with all the food he needed, and he does very little cultivating. For that reason other more industrious races, such as the Hindus who were imported here to work on the sugar plantations, have taken a firm root on Fijian soil ; and it is only a question of time before the original Fijian race, like the American Indians, will be in a small minority, and forced to live on reservations. Indeed, were it not for the white man's government, the natives would have sold all their land long ago.

One day I was introduced to Ratu Bulah, a big native chief. He is over six feet tall, and of imposing appearance : but he spends his time loafing about the town, welcoming visitors and showing them the sights. He took me through the Street of All Nations, and pointed out places where I could get things cheaply. " Why pay half a crown for a meal in a hotel," said he, " if in a Chinese restaurant you can get a good meal for a shilling or even sixpence ? Why buy fruit in shops when you can get it for half the price in the native market ? "

As we were passing a hotel I said : " I don't drink, but can I give you one ? "

" Sure," said the chief. " We natives are not allowed in the bar, but give me the ninepence, and I will get it all right at the back door."

A few days later he introduced me to a Tongan chief who had lately come to Fiji : and I asked Ratu Bulah if he had given a feast to welcome his distinguished visitor.

" No," he replied sadly, " cannot do it nowadays —no money."

And, indeed, later on I saw his " distinguished visitor " loading coal on a lighter.

There is another and worse type of native degradation which has been created by the tourist traffic—worse, because it thrives by perverting what used to be the conspicuous South Sea virtues of kindness and hospitality. Thank goodness it is not very common as yet. I refer to the over-friendly Samoan : who meets you at the steamer, is eager to shake hands, beaming all over in welcoming smiles. He dotes on you : he loves you more than he would his brother : and there is nothing in the world that he would not do for you. If you have any dirty clothes his wife will wash them for you ; and should you do the honour

85

of calling at his home he will have a dinner prepared for you.

Naturally the tourist does not want to impose on
the kindness of this charming type, and probably
evades the call at his home. Next time the Samoan
meets him he laments aloud that the white man
did not turn up : he had counted on his coming,
and he had spent two shillings on a chicken for
the feast—and now that is all gone to waste.

Probably the tourist reimburses him for the pretended loss ; and that is only the beginning of the
trickle of money from one pocket to the other.
Sometimes the Samoan's wife is ill and needs a
bottle of medicine : sometimes his father has died,
and the funeral expenses have fallen upon him
suddenly. How is the tourist to resist this kind of
confidence-trick when his pocket is emptied in the
name of brotherly love, and the leech professes
himself ready to do anything in the world for his
dear friend ?

But it is not only an inherent decadence which is
wrong with the natives of Fiji. Ratu Bulah spoke
truly when he said there was no longer any money
for feasting, or for the time-honoured amenities of
the independent native life. The Fijian native is
terribly impoverished.

It is often easier to see the working of an economic
law when it is applied on a small scale than on a

large one : and nowhere would it be easier to see the strangling effect of high tariffs than in the economic life of Fiji. If they export bananas to Australia, the Australian tariffs are so high that tariff and freight between them send up the price ten times. You may say that it does not matter to the Fijian—it is the Australian who has to pay highly for his bananas. But it does matter ; for if the Fijian native wants to buy some printed cotton for his loin-cloth, he can only buy it from Australia with the bananas he exports. Consequently he has to pay ten times the value of the cotton in bananas. Then again, the fantastic price to which the bananas are forced up before they reach the consumer has reacted very seriously on the volume of the market. The demand has shrunk, but the supply has not shrunk proportionately ; and consequently the price of bananas at Suva has dropped from five shillings to two shillings a case. This fall in the price paid to the producer is of little avail to lower the retail price, because the original cost of the bananas in any case is but a minute portion of their final cost—but it is death to the producer, for it leaves him only a fraction of the original amount to spend on imports. And of that fraction, when he spends it on imports, how much is eaten up by his own government's import duties, by harbour dues and

licences ! How little goes to the cotton operative
in the far country !

Indeed, who benefits by these high tariffs it
would be hard to say. By making the prices high
for Fijian goods in Australia, and for Australian
goods in Fiji, it is not only the consumers that
suffer : the whole volume of trade suffers, and in
consequence the returns of the taxes themselves
are reduced—and so the governments suffer too !

An acquaintance in Fiji once asked me—for he
had observed that I had freed myself in an uncommon way from the usual toils of a modern
civilized life—whether I would not like to go
native, and live in Fiji as the natives do. Seeing
that impoverishment, I could only answer, " No."
Moreover, in my heart I knew there was another
reason. There is something in those natives which
makes them accept life without a struggle : there
is something in me which makes the necessity of
struggle seem the foremost thing in life itself. I
could never accept life passively as the boulder
accepts the stream which splashes over it. My
nature was rather that of the salmon which swims
against the stream, and who, when he reaches a
rapid or waterfall or other difficult point, knows
that he must leap it with every atom of strength
in his being.

And yet how much are these tendencies racial ?

va military band
ie heights, Island of Naitamba

How much are they merely climatic and geographical? I spent only seven weeks in Suva, but already by the end of that time I began to feel " Malua fever "—the disease of procrastination and disinclination to work—creeping over me.

For hours sometimes I would lounge in the shade of a tree : or would stroll out on to the reef to watch the animal life there. The little yellow sand-crab had a particular fascination for me. Brandishing his only claw—which is as big as himself—one would advance against another as if about to give battle. But these battles seldom came off. If one crab was the smaller he would give way and retire. But if two crabs of the same size met, then there was no giving way! In the twinkling of an eye their claws would interlock, and they would wrestle until one would be thrown over on to his back. Once he had taken such a fall he gave in : got on to his feet as best he could, and trundled away.

There was a crane, too, who used to come to the reef every morning. He would stroll majestically in the shallows which abounded with little fish, and then presently he would begin to dance. It was a regular Highland Fling, accompanied by the flapping of his wings. It terrified the little fish, who would hurry away and hide in the mud

—from which presently he would pick them out with his long bill.

Another curiosity of the place was the mangrove-tree, which propagates itself by cuttings without the gardener's aid. I had often noticed spindly sticks, nine to ten inches long, floating on the water ; but one day I found what happened to these. Presently the water washed them up against the rock, and wedged them into crevices—whereupon they immediately threw out roots, and soon were shooting leaves !—Was I perhaps just such a stick, floating on the ocean, now washed up on the shore and about to throw out roots in the same manner ? I began to feel that if ever I was to leave Fiji, it must be soon.

The leisure, however, had given me time for contemplation, and had not been wholly spent in idle day-dreaming. I had been talking one day with some of my new friends about the hazards of such sea-faring as mine, and had pointed out to them that if these hazards did not matter to me they mattered to nobody in the world, for there was no one in the world to whom my life was of any value. At this I saw their eyes grow moist, and they told me that what I had said might once have been true, but was true no longer.

How could my heart help but warm at such

kindliness ? What had I done to deserve the sympathy of these people ? I had made no efforts to win their friendship : but they were so nice towards me that I could not help but love them back. Partly it was this revelation to me of human kindness, which reminded me of that boundless kindness of God of which it is but a reflection : partly it was the answers which my prayers had received, which turned me to think seriously about religion. I had a Bible, and took to reading it. One day I opened it at the curse in the thirtieth verse of the twenty-eighth chapter of Deuteronomy : " Thou shalt betroth a wife and another man shall live with her. Thou shall build a house and shall not dwell therein. Thou shalt plant a vineyard and shall not use the fruit thereof." The words struck me as a blow between the eyes. Could any words have described more aptly my own life ? Was I then under a curse from Heaven ? A curse none the less sure, though my ears had never heard it uttered ? What had I done, that any curse should be laid upon me ? I read on, and verse forty-five gave me the answer : I had not kept God's commandments. For almost twenty-five years I had been engrossed in the battle for life, fighting for my own hand, and giving God's commandments no thought. For almost twenty-five years I had been in pursuit of happiness—

ignorant that there is no more certain way of failing to find it. And yet—so the answers to my prayers and the kindness shown me by these people told me—the curse might be lifted at once, did I but mend my ways.

My safe passage across the ocean had taught me one lesson, and Fiji had taught me another : but I felt now the need of the ocean once more, so that in complete isolation from the rest of mankind I might consider undisturbed what steps must be taken to free my soul from the trammels of so many wasted years, and set it once more upon the right path.

*   *   *

At last my boat was fixed up. The crack had been repaired, and a fine new centre-board had been presented to me by the government officers of Fiji. I had fixed new stays, new running gear, and had repainted her. In fact, *Elaine* was now a finer boat than when I left Sydney. She was also better equipped ; for kind friends had presented me with a spare sail, a compass, and a barometer, and a proper set of charts.

The hurricane season had already begun when I arrived in Fiji, and now it was nearly at its end : so I decided on the 20th April as my day of departure. Regretfully I said good-bye to my many friends, and stowed on board the parcels of cake, jam, and provisions that they gave me.

On the day I set sail a number of schoolboys were assembled to watch my departure. One of the teachers said, " Mr. Rebell wants a cabin-boy ; any of you willing to go put up your hand."

A forest of hands went up. When at last I had boarded my boat, which was swinging at anchor just off the shore, they gave me three of the heartiest cheers I had ever heard. And not long after I was riding once more on the boundless deep.

CHAPTER IX

*Night Sailing in Narrow Waters—Saved by a Dream—The
" Date Line "—Arrival at Naitamba—A Hospitable Planter
—Eden with Three Eves—Another Picnic—Gentle Betty—I
Run Away to Sea*

THERE are over two hundred and fifty islands in
the Fiji group, let alone reefs : and so, with head-
winds and unknown currents, night-sailing was
particularly dangerous. I nearly came to grief the
very first night I left Suva. I had set my course for
the East Channel, which should have given me an
unobstructed run ; but I had not made sufficient
allowance for currents, or for a shift in the wind.

At about midnight I had a curious dream. I
dreamed that my boat was making straight for a pile,
which rose out of the water a short way in front.
The fear of an impending collision was so violent
as to wake me, and on looking out I was astounded
to see—only a quarter of a mile to starboard—the
blinking light of the Naselai lighthouse. Right in
front of me a white line of breakers revealed a submerged reef. I quickly threw over the helm, and
did not go below again till well clear of the danger.

The odd thing is that never before while at sea had I dreamed of sailing—much less of running into an obstruction while sailing ! All my dreams had been either fantastic, or of the shore : this was the very first time that I had dreamed anything of the kind. And yet the dream had come at the very moment when it could save my life.

* * *

It was among these Fijian islands that I crossed the " date line," and so experienced that phenomenon so puzzling to land-lubbers of having an extra day in my year. It happened near noon on Sunday, 24th April : so I simply struck out the date in my log-book, and wrote " Saturday 23rd April." Thus this particular week I had one and a half Saturdays, and one and a half Sundays.

* * *

Nor was it only at night that sailing was sometimes dangerous. While in Fijian waters I often came across drifting tree-trunks, and should have been stove in if I had run into one hard. During my whole voyage, I found my bob-stay broken at the bottom shackle no less than three times. But whether this was through hitting a tree-trunk, or what other derelict, I could not say : for so much of my sailing was " blind " and automatic : at least nine-tenths of the time no look-out was kept.

For four days after leaving Suva I was tacking against head-winds and dodging reefs and islands. In such dangerous sailing I got very little sleep. My boat too had been so long on the slip at Suva that she had dried, and the joints had opened up ; and so she was leaking rather badly.

I had intended that my first port of call should be Apia in Samoa ; but now, when I came to a certain island called Naitamba, I resolved to land and get some rest, and have the seams attended to.

As I drew in towards the lee of the island, where a few launches were swinging at anchor, it was soon apparent that this was no native settlement. The regular rows of palm-trees growing up the hillside proclaimed it to be a plantation : and across the still air there carried the mooing of cows, the gabble of turkeys, the clatter of geese and the crowing of cocks. Then among the brush on the shore I spied a girlish figure, and caught a flash of a European dress.

When I had anchored, a native boy approached in a rowing-boat and asked me in good English if I wished to go ashore to see the planter : so I went with him.

We landed on a concrete jetty, at the foot of which were drying-racks and sheds for copra. The planter's residence stood in its own grounds a little farther inland, the kitchen and dormitories being in separate buildings. And farther still I could see the houses of the native labourers.

Mr. Hennings was the planter : an amiable gentleman of about fifty. He came out to meet me, and when I had explained the reason for my call said that he had read about me in the papers, and would render me every assistance he could. " You can put up at the guest-cottage," he said. " Or if you would rather sleep on your boat, you can have my dinghy to come and go. Please make yourself at home at my house. There is plenty to read there, if you care for reading. The family is seldom indoors except for meals ; but we eat at eight, at one, at four and at six ; so please come whenever you hear the Lalo (wooden drum)."

He then introduced me to the family. His wife was a cultured German lady ; and they had three lovely daughters—Elizabeth, Sophia and Myra— their ages 19, 17, and 10.

I found the Henningses most charming people. At first I felt awkward at intruding myself so abruptly on the hospitality of a private family circle ; but they let me feel no scruples, and made it plain that I was welcome—it was, they said, the regular South Sea custom.

So I spent ten days on Naitamba, enjoying the

company of these people and their well-cooked
meals : and explored the island and the plantation.
Naitamba is only four square miles in extent ; but
it is quite rugged in places, and reaches a height of
over four hundred feet above sea-level.   There was
a native settlement here, once : but their chief
became so disgusted with the character of his subjects that he deported them to another island, and
sold this one to the Europeans.   Consequently the
whole of it now belongs to the Henningses.   Mr.
Hennings employs permanently about forty natives
picking copra.   He has a herd of three hundred
cattle, and quite a number of other domestic
animals.

And fowls.   Poultry roamed at large, and more
died of old age than of the knife.   However, whenever Mrs. Hennings required a chicken for the
table she pointed out to her setter the one she
wanted, and ordered, "Catch him."   Before the
words were fairly out of her mouth, the dog brought
the chicken to her hand.

Coconuts, as I saw when I drove round the island
in a motor-truck, were lying everywhere in the
plantation.   If Mr. Hennings could get a cent for
every coconut he owned he would be a millionaire,
I reckon !   Bananas, pineapples, pawpaws, and
other fruit grow here too : but mainly for domestic
consumption, not for export.

A good deal of the island is still in its wild state, and it was arranged that on Sunday Betty and Sophie should take me for a trip round it. When I turned up at the rendezvous I found them all togged up : large stetson hat, white cotton shirt, khaki shorts, and sand-shoes. And each was armed with a large knife—as fine a pair of Amazons as ever made a mere man's knees knock. " What are the knives for ? " I asked : " attack, or defence ? "

" Oh, no," they said : " just for opening coconuts, if we happen to feel thirsty, and cutting jungle."

We drove as far as the truck would take us, and then did some mountaineering on foot. There was a fine view from the heights : islands one hundred miles away could be seen and distinguished. But those heights took some reaching. At one place we had to climb an improvised ladder on to a rocky ledge—the ladder was an old dead tree-trunk, with bits of wood nailed on for rungs, dating from native days. How long it had been there nobody knew : how much longer it would last before breaking and dropping someone a hundred feet down the hillside, no one seemed to care.

In native days all funerals went up this ladder : for they used to carry their dead to a tunnel or cave higher up in the hill. Nobody knows now where

E

this cave is, although we spent some time looking for it.

On our way back Betty pointed out to me various peculiar kinds of trees. One of them bleeds red if you cut its bark : from another we picked wodoo nuts, which have a tasty kernel when you split them open. Then there was a kind of wild, very acid passion-fruit.

We had been wandering like this for a couple of hours, and the day was rather warm : so when we got back to the truck we opened some green coconuts for a drink.

That was an art at which Sophie excelled : natives included, I have never seen anyone so dexterous at opening a nut. A few deft strokes with the large knife slashed away the husk, and left a neat opening from which you could sip the delicious contents. Then should you wish to eat the thin layer of still jelly-like kernel, another stroke of her knife laid the nut right open : a chip from the husk supplied a serviceable spoon, and the feast was spread.

I remember how my own clumsy attempts at Suva had evoked the derisive laughter of the natives : and though I had improved greatly since, I could not match Champion Sophie. Though she was the younger of the two she was larger and stronger than Betty, and well on the way to becoming her father's right hand on the plantation : for in addition she was an adept at book-keeping, and could drive the lorry and the motor-launch.

Betty had more inclination for home and garden. On one of the rocky ledges, during our meanderings, she had spied a wild lily in bloom. She pulled it up, bulb and all, to take home. It was pathetic to see the care which she took of it. When she got home she took it to her mother in delight : asked in what favoured nook the treasure should be planted. Her mother merely glanced at it and said, " I do not think much of these forest lilies : the narcissi we have are ever so much prettier," and Betty stole away with a hurt look in her eyes.

A couple of days later Betty asked me what I thought of the island. I told her it was the nearest approach to Paradise I had ever seen.

" You would not think so if you lived here longer."

" Why ? " I answered.

" You would miss the world. We are so isolated here ; mail only once a month, and hardly any callers. I think we are getting fossilized here."

" No, Betty," I said. " The world and its strife would not give you any satisfaction, or make you happier. Some day perhaps one person will : but till then you are better off in this Eden. Is there anybody in the outside world yet for whom you really care ? "

" No," she said. " Lately we spent nine months travelling in Europe, and made many acquaintances : but there is no one I really regret."

With everyone else busy at this or that, I could not be content to remain idle : so I asked Mr. Hennings to make me useful. A few piano-keys were sticking, the gramophone needed oiling, some lamps would not burn, and there were clocks and watches that would not go. So I set to, and in a couple of days had them all in running order. Then I decided to push on.

" I am sorry you are going," said Betty. " We were planning another picnic next Sunday—on horseback this time. We thought you would enjoy it."

I surely would have ; but if I stayed here much longer, I feared that perhaps my journey would never get completed.

And indeed this was true, for I was beginning to think too much of gentle Betty. So I said good-bye to this kindly family, took aboard the scones, eggs, meat and bananas they gave me, and next morning pushed off again once more to sea.

CHAPTER X

The Fijis Left Behind—Gales and Head Winds—The Lost Infant—Fish and Birds—May 24th : Arrival at Apia (Samoa)—Native Society To-day—The Mau Movement— The New Zealand Mandate—Tariffs Again

I MIGHT decide in my wisdom that the sooner I left this island the better : but the winds thought otherwise : and for a whole day I was becalmed in the lee of Naitamba. But at last a breeze freshened and soon I dropped Wailangi Lala, the last of the Fiji Islands, astern. The breeze now stiffened to a gale. I had to take in all sail, and for a day I felt anxious lest I should be blown back on to the dangerous reefs of Fiji.

After the gale subsided I was soon making good headway. But a few days later a squall stole up on me so unexpectedly that the boat heeled over before I could get in sail, and was in danger of swamping. That, indeed, is the worst feature of ocean sailing in an open boat : a man can never be wholly at ease. Day and night, asleep or awake, you must be on the *qui vive*, ready to jump at a moment's notice when some sudden emergency

103

arises. Consider for how many months I had to remain thus on tenterhooks ! If it had not been for this one thing, perhaps I should have enjoyed my sailing more keenly than I did.

Anyone who has read many accounts of single-handed voyages will have noticed that for the most part these voyages were from east to west. This is not accidental : it is to take advantage of the prevailing winds, which, especially in the Tropics, blow in that direction. My voyage, on the other hand, was to the eastward as well as northward : hence the little progress I often made ; for I was generally battling against head-winds. There is an exasperation in finding the wind blowing always bung out of that point of the compass you wish to head for : an exasperation which is cumulative, grows as the same conditions hold from week to week.

It is very seldom, however, that the wind blows absolutely steadily from the same point day and night : at sunset and sunrise it usually shifts a point or two. If you are lucky enough to be able to make use of this, sailing on one tack by day and the other by night, of course you get to windward somewhat better.

Such was my first ten days' sailing after I had left the Fiji group, when I came to the half-way island called by the South Sea Islanders Niuafoo

which means " The Lost Infant " (the higher civili-
zations of Europe, however, have named it Tin Can
Island). I passed it quite close. It is a hilly little
island, two or three miles across ; and even on the
lee side the surf was heavily breaking on a rocky
shore. I could see an old white-washed stone
church there, and a couple of graves with big white
crosses over them. The church looked dilapidated,
and the corrugated iron which had evidently been
its roof now covered a large native hut near by.
A few more huts were visible in the woods along
the shore, and smoke was rising in the hills. Somehow it was an uninviting-looking place : and though
with the approach of dusk two big flares—probably
leading marks—were lit upon the shore, I was not
tempted to put in. For I now had a fair wind from
the south-east : and it needs considerable temp-
tation for a sailor to put into land when, after many
days beating to windward, a fair wind at last blows.
That fair wind carried me the whole way to Savaii.

The ocean between Fiji and Samoa was swarming
with fish. It was a pretty sight, at sunset, to watch
schools of bonitos, pursued by some enemy, jump-
ing out of the water simultaneously and repeatedly.
My only regret was that none of them ever
jumped into my boat. Flying fishes, however,
frequently fell on board—and before long would

be sizzling in the frying-pan, for they are very good eating. Schools of smaller fish, too, would continually follow my boat, and travel with it ; some ahead, some behind : and it was curious to see some of them attempting to imitate the rotating motion of my log-spinner. I suppose they thought it a new discovery in the art of swimming : but if so, they made little success at it. All this while I could catch as many fish for the pot as I liked.

As well as these friendly creatures I had certain less welcome followers. Sharks would pursue the boat for days, and nibble at the spinner of the log, so that again and again I had to haul it aboard and straighten out its aluminium blades. I dislike sharks for company : I hated their beady eyes, which seemed to watch my every movement.

I had a four-pronged harpoon with a long handle ; so when a seven-foot shark got too close I jabbed at its body with it. I might as well have tried to puncture a motor-tyre—he was so tough. I had another go at its head : the harpoon stuck this time, the shark jerked round, I hung on to the handle : the handle broke, and away he went. And for all I know he is still racing through the ocean with my tiara on his head.

I then made a really sharp spear, and with that was able to give the sharks all the discouragement they needed.

106

And birds. A big grey and white booby-bird came aboard one evening, and perched on the boom. He stuck to that perch for quite a long while, though the jolting of the boom made it somewhat of a balancing feat. When I tried to touch him with my hand he did not fly away—he only squawked and tried to peck me.

Stormy petrels—tiny little birds, the size of a swallow—could be seen daily flying over the waves. It was always a wonder to me how so small a bird could exist hundreds of miles away from land.

When I had at length rounded Savaii on the north, it was a beat again to reach Apia. 24th May was a breezy day : and I crowded on all sail, so as to reach Apia before dusk. The choppy head-seas sent the spray mast-high : it fell on board in showers, and I had to bail the boat every two hours.

Gradually the town of Apia rose out of the sea. First a white church appeared, then the roofs of houses, and presently a whole string of buildings lining the sides of the harbour.

What a peaceful place it seemed ! What an enchanting contrast of light and shade ! The sun had set now behind the mountain, and a twinkling of lights appeared in the town. As I entered the harbour the ocean swell gave way to a calm. There were long-boats practising, and from one there came a rhythmical drumming on a paraffin-can. As they drew abreast I asked, " Is there any good place to anchor here ? "

" Yes.   Follow us.—Where are you from ? "

" Sydney and Suva."

" We had been expecting you.   Where are you bound ? "

" California."

" That is if you get there ! " they jeered.

" Quite so," I replied tranquilly.

In Fiji I had been advised against going to Apia, for the natives there, I was told, are rude towards Europeans.   I wondered how they would behave towards myself now.   Anyway, I anchored near the jetty, had my tea and turned in.   I did not go ashore, however : for I was not going to risk again a scolding such as I had had from the medical officer at Suva.   So early next morning I hoisted the yellow flag, and as I was getting my breakfast ready the Harbour Master came in a launch and towed me up to the jetty.   Here the doctor was waiting and examined my Suva clearance-papers. They passed me, and told me that I could tie up on the other side of the jetty if I liked.

My boat was already exciting a lot of interest, and (just as at Suva) people came up abruptly to ply me with questions and stare at the boat.   At first I was in doubt how friendly they were going to

108

prove ; but I did not remain in doubt for long. Somebody passed me some fresh fish on a plate, and some bananas ; and then they all began. Another brought me a plaited palm hat for a present, and many of them asked me to go to their houses for a meal.

There is a great difference between the Samoan and the Fijian native. In Samoa there is little of the dark-skinned, frizzy-haired Melanesian stock. There the straight-haired Polynesian type predominates, with lighter complexions : indeed, many Samoans might easily be mistaken for Portuguese or Spaniards. Their dress too is different. In Fiji, as a rule, the men wear the short lava-lava, reaching only to their knees : but here you can hardly tell a man from a woman at a little distance, since both wear the lava-lava right down to the ankle. I do not know whether this is an old custom, or part of the effeminateness of a new generation : a generation which no longer has the fortitude to have its pants tattooed (as formerly) upon the skin. In olden times that painful custom was considered a test of manhood. An untattooed Samoan was not considered a man : one with the job half done— one, that is to say, who had been unable to stick it out—was branded for ever as a coward.

I was impressed too at first by the graceful and indeed queenly bearing of some of the native girls.

109

But if you wish to retain this impression of aristocratic grace it does not do to watch them for too long : for sooner or later you would be bound to see them spit in the best sailor fashion, or wipe their noses with their fingers.

They are a genial, bantering race : it is not often that you fail to hear light-hearted laughter on one side of you or the other. A race, too, much given to horseplay. I remember noticing two young men with a girl one day on the jetty. She was dressed up to the nines, in a silk lava-lava and with her hair fashionably done. She was protesting shrilly : and well she might, for her two swains were trying to pitch her into the sea : and indeed, this they presently did.

The native race still predominates here ; though there is a sprinkling of Chinese, Japanese and Indians. There are only a couple of hundred Europeans : but there are plenty of half-castes. The colour-line is not drawn so clearly here as in Suva, and the relations between whites and natives are far more cordial.

I met many white men here (including an English officer), with refined and cultured native wives who had proved as fine life-partners as one could wish for. Indeed, nowhere in the world does the European young lady meet with more competition in the marriage-market than in Samoa.

Life in Apia

Apia is a small place : almost a one-street-town : and some of the wooden houses look as if they needed but a good stiff breeze to blow them away. The native huts differ from the Fijian in that they are entirely open on all sides, with mats that can be let down to windward to keep out the wind or rain. Therefore Samoan family life is normally open to the gaze of every passer-by ; and it is quite a common sight to see a woman squatting in a native house giving suck to a baby. But the morals of these people are good, and one hears little of conjugal disloyalty.

Outside Apia the native houses are grouped in villages, and each village possesses a communal plantation where they grow their coconuts, bananas, taro, breadfruit, and pawpaws. Each village has a hereditary Matai, or Elder, who supervises both the production and distribution of food. He allots the different public tasks, and generally looks after his own and the community's welfare. In most villages it is customary for a plot of the plantation ground to be ear-marked for every man, woman and child in the village (I was once offered such a plot of ground myself, if I would like to stay).

Thus, the patriarchal or matriarchal order still prevails here : but it is beginning to break up in contact with the European wage-system. Some of the natives have found employment in shops or offices, and then have refused to put their earnings into the common family chest. For they naturally find they can get more comfort and pleasure by keeping their money for themselves. In consequence they have dropped out of the family ; and henceforth must pay for any food they eat.

Lately, however, an opposite tendency has made its appearance : the " Mau " movement, which was an attempt to consolidate all the villages under a somewhat communistic government. This movement naturally clashed with the Powers That Be— the Government of New Zealand, that is to say, which has a mandate over Samoa : and some blood was shed.

Seeing the Samoans are poorly equipped with warships and machine-guns, naturally the blood that was shed was chiefly Samoan blood.

Discontent, though no longer open, still exists, however : for the yoke of the white man lies heavy on the native. Not in the visible form of direct taxation, but in the more hidden (but none the less pinching) form of tariffs and customs-dues. It is the same tale as I had to tell about Fiji.

Why should a mail-boat, entering the absolutely natural harbour of Apia, where there is not even a wharf to tie up to, have to pay fifty pounds a day in harbour dues ? Naturally they have to recoup it from the freights they charge—and thus it is the

Samoan who pays those harbour dues in the end. But that is not all he has to pay. There is a twenty-five per cent. duty on imports ; and also a heavy export duty on copra and bananas, the island's principal produce. As in Fiji, these burdens upon trade have done their part towards reducing trade to a standstill. The slump is fearful, and many traders and planters have been knocked out altogether— some even being reduced to beachcombers. And yet, under it all, native cheerfulness and hospitality remain the same. Nobody is ever refused a meal here, and if the host has anything which the guest fancies it is his for the asking.

There used to be a custom here for one whole village to go to visit another and be feasted by them, and then to return home loaded with presents. But this custom the government has succeeded in discouraging—since under that government's beneficent tutelage the native economy can no longer afford such extravagant pleasures.

To a certain extent perhaps this discontent in British Samoa can be traced to American sources. Barely fifty miles away there lies the island of Tutuila, or American Samoa, which contains the naval base of Pango Pango. Thanks to the American gold which has been splashed there the Tutuila natives are completely spoilt, and expect wages on an American scale. Consequently the American

Samoan native enjoys a higher standard of living than does his brother, the British Samoan. So it is no wonder the other is dissatisfied ; for the New Zealand Government does not conspicuously value its Samoan mandate as an opportunity for the spending of British gold. Rather she values it as providing a compulsory market for British goods : a haven of refuge for superfluous officials : and a source of cheap native labour.

Nor is there much love lost between the two neighbouring governments, who carry on a war-fare of pin-pricks against each other. Whenever a British inter-island boat, no matter how small, enters Pango Pango, it has to pay harbour and other fees to American officialdom : and whenever the American boat comes to Apia, heavy harbour dues must be paid to British officialdom. The Samoan looks on at this, and wonders that two great and indeed respectable governments cannot live side by side on better terms.

But, as I have indicated, the resources of native economy are so rich in Samoa that it would take a more ingenious government than the present one wholly to impoverish the natives. A few feet of ground will grow all that a man needs for his food : and all the work he needs to do is to keep it clear of weeds. One breadfruit tree will supply a family all the year round with those large canteloupe-

114

like fruit that when steamed make an excellent substitute for mealy potatoes. Then there is taro —a lily which grows in the swamps—with its parsnip-like roots ; and the coconut palm, which requires no cultivation at all, and which will grow almost anywhere—even where the ground-water is actually salt. It puzzles me how the palm manages to prevent the salt finding its way into the nuts : even at the edge of the sea the nuts will always supply a refreshing and nourishing drink. The uses of the coconut are endless. Coconut cream may be extracted from the grated kernel— one coconut will make a bottleful : and when mixed with sea water and flavoured with chili onions it makes a most delicious sauce. With this sauce even a meal of nothing but taro is enjoyable.

Then there are the bananas and the pawpaws, which also grow almost anywhere. All you have to do is to prevent other trees and creepers from choking them.

But the Samoans do not live entirely on the products of the soil. Like most of the South Sea islanders they spend a lot of time fishing or fish-spearing ; and it is surprising, too, to see the variety of sea-food that can be gathered off a reef—fish, clams, crabs, oysters, octopuses and edible seaweed.

Such is the vast larder of Nature, the door of

which for the Samoan stands ever open. And when he has chosen his food he needs no expensive kitchen range or gas-oven to cook it. A few stones heated in a fire are laid at the bottom of a hole in the ground : then the food, wrapped in large leaves, is placed in the hot stones, and the bundle covered with more leaves and stones. Within an hour everything is perfectly cooked.

CHAPTER XI

*Samoa—Diseases and Pests Introduced from Abroad—
" Gone Native "—A Belgian Beach-comber—A Samoan
Princess—The Native Point of View—Stevenson's Grave—
A Lovely Little Half-caste—The Importance of Shaving—
Farewell, Samoa !*

I SAID that it would need more ingenuity than the
present Government possesses to slam the door of
this vast natural larder in the natives' faces : but
the white man none the less is on the way to
achieve this end by accident. For it was presum-
ably by accident that he introduced the parasites of
elephantiasis into the island. Now they lurk in
the taro swamps, and taro cultivation is therefore
become somewhat dangerous. Again, it was as a
garden plant that the mile-a-minute creeper was
introduced : which now can completely overrun a
plantation in a few weeks, unless coolies are constantly employed to battle with it—coolies who,
the moment they finish at one end of the plantation, have to begin again at the other. The
story of the mimosa plant is the same : that too
was introduced for the charm of its appearance, but
has become a weed, costing the island thousands
of man-hours of labour every month.

117

I met a countryman of mine, a fellow-Latvian, in Apia : and he took me out to see his plantation. He had about thirty acres of cacao-trees in full bearing : but he had to keep a gang of coolies constantly at work to fight the imported weeds. Cacao-trees must be kept quite clear if they are to flourish : and at that time, during the slump, cacao was the only product whose export was at all profitable.

My fellow-countryman opened a bottle of gin to celebrate my visit : and since I do not touch drink myself he had to finish the bottle alone in my honour. As politely as I could I told him that finishing the bottle in one sitting was in my opinion carrying the requirements of courtesy a little further than necessary : but he disagreed. This life, he said, would drive anyone to drink.

" Look at my wife," he said, pointing at that lady. " Wouldn't she drive you to drink ? Look at her w—w—w—waist ! It would take you three days just to walk round her.—How can I ever go back to Latvia and show my people *that* ? And yet, time was she was as slim as a reed. All the native girls are like that : slim when they are young, but as they get older——"

Finishing the sentence beggared his imagination, and he filled himself another glass.

" Swim," he said suddenly, " they can swim

118

like fish. She could swim round you in circles even now." And he relapsed into muttering again.

" Married ? " he said, becoming coherent again : " well no, we are not exactly married. Here, where a woman does not depend on a man for her living, there is no need for strict marriage laws. Live together for a bit, and then separate—that is the way of it. Well, some day, perhaps, I will send her home to her village like I sent the others. But then, what about my two girls ? The elder one would pass for a European : I might keep her. But the other's the living spit of her mama : have to be back to the village for her too, if I was ever to show myself in Latvia again ! "

He then drained the bottle carefully, and swallowed the last few drops.

" So you are going back to the homeland ? " he said. " Well, perhaps I will follow you. I long to see it again, if only once. The wintry blanket of snow, the frozen river, the sombre pine, the bare branches : I would love to feel the nip of frosty air in the morning again, after this eternal summer ! And the springtime ! Everything coming to life again—field and tree covered with new green and new blossoms. Yes," he went on, " I am going home : sure as fate I am going home —some day ! "

He told me he had two sisters living at home—
old maids (for forty per cent. of Latvia's male
population was killed in the war.) He seemed
very sure that he would go back to see them—with
his elder daughter—" some day."

But I knew he never would. Drink had too
strong a hold on him, and " malua fever." Nor
was he ever likely to send his portly wife back to
her village : for it was quite plain that affection
tied them much more closely than any marriage
bond could have done. He would have been lost
without her : and she, without him, as lost as an
old nannie parted from her baby.

*   *   *

Two or three nights later I listened to another
tale of woe from a European, a Belgian beach-
comber. It was a sad tale indeed (whether true
or not) of how he had been cheated by his employer
of nine months' wages, and how the employer then
lied about him to the police, thus getting him into
everybody's bad books. But I could not help feeling that a man who was got down permanently by
such a thing must deserve, to some extent at least,
his place in the bad books of solid citizens. This
man was now placidly awaiting the day when he
should have proved himself so much of a nuisance

120

to the island that the Government would pay him fifty pounds to take himself elsewhere.

But such white civilized society was not the only society in which I moved during my visit to Apia. I had my boat ashore, and was cleaning and painting the bottom one day when a young native lady (evidently of some rank, for there was a servant-girl holding a parasol over her) came towards me and said :

" Allow me to introduce myself. My name is Leofa Semeunutafa Tuisila, and I am the daughter of the Chief of Apia."

She said that her mother (for it was her mother who was the chief, or Matai) wanted to meet me, and invited me to supper that night. The servant-girl would come to show me the way.

The chief's house stood in a clearing just at the back of the town, and differed from the other native houses in that it was carefully built and nicely finished inside, with a high raised wooden floor.

Leofa's mother, a distinguished and refined native of middle age, was dressed in European fashion. She greeted me very hospitably and invited me to take all my meals at their house as long as I remained in Apia, if that was my wish.

When supper was served only the Matai and myself sat down at table. Not expecting a five-course dinner I allowed myself to be too good a trencherman with the entrées, only to find myself somewhat in difficulties when roast chicken and then sweets followed them. The cooking was European, and the meals served in European style with only one exception—that the plates for the hot dishes were stone cold.

After supper I learned that my hostess was the only child of Semeunutafa. That renowned chieftain had distinguished himself in a hurricane that hit Apia over thirty years ago by saving the lives of many of the crew of a wrecked American warship, and so had earned the official thanks of the American Government. Leofa again was the only child of the present chief ; and so would succeed her mother when the time came. Leofa's twenty-first birthday, which would fall in two months' time, was therefore to be celebrated with a great feast to which the Governor himself would be invited. A gathering of the patriarchs was to be held the next Wednesday at which arrangements for this feast were to be made. Would I care to be present ?

I said that I would.

Wednesday came, and the meeting was held in one of the native huts. All present sat on mats leaning against the roof-posts, and the Matai addressed them for about an hour. What she said I do not know : but she was plainly a fluent and powerful speaker.

Then, when the speech-making was over, about twenty baskets of food were brought in : taro, breadfruit, fish, pork, and chicken : and were divided among the various families or houses represented at the meeting. Each portion also included a tin of corned beef (which the natives oddly enough call " pea soup "), the only imported food for which they have acquired a taste.

Being invited to call frequently at the Matai's house, I agreed to do so on condition they cooked me no more European meals, but let me take pot-luck : for in my heart of hearts I much preferred native cooking.

Sometimes when I was there the Matai herself was absent, and Leofa entertained me. She was a full-blooded native, of course, and proud of it. By native standards she would be considered a beauty, for she was full of face, and fat right down to the heels : strong and big-boned : a worthy grand-daughter of a great grandsire.

In her pride of race she had little but contempt for Europeans (half-castes she disregarded totally). She had been to college at Auckland in New Zealand for a couple of years : and the whites she had met there, she said, were far inferior to the Samoan natives both in hospitality and in sense of dignity. What was she to think of white men whom she found cadging from her in the streets, selling newspapers and ties, standing in bread-lines ? Or of those others whose doings filled the newspapers—those who spent their time robbing one another, murdering, raping and thieving ?

I tried to tell her that to judge the white races by the trash she met in city streets was to misjudge them. " You will find hospitable white people," I said, " all over the world ; especially among peasants, and others who grow their own food. But in cities where food is an article for which all expect to have to pay hard-earned cash there is little room for hospitality. To practise it would simply be an invitation to every kind of cadger, loafer and idler, every parasite and criminal. You simply cannot afford, in a modern city, to practise such a primitive virtue as hospitality."

But she was hard to convince.

Leofa's accomplishments were many. She could play the piano : and not only used she to play the organ in the native church, but also to preach at daily prayer-meetings in her own home.

Those prayer meetings ended the day. After them everyone turned in—if you could call it by that name, when all a Samoan does is to lie on a mat on the floor with a hard, polished, bamboo head-rest for a pillow.

* * *

Was there no white man for whom the natives could or did feel respect and good-will? Well, there was one; and I went on pilgrimage to him.

It was a three-mile walk up-hill past Vailima, where Stevenson died, to the little clearing in the forest where his grave lies. The respect and affection which he inspired were genuine enough. Stevenson died in 1894. He had only been in the island for four years; but he had proved so strong a friend to the Samoan that when he died sixty sturdy natives, who acknowledged him their chief, carried him to the precipitous peak of Vaea and buried him there. That was nearly forty years ago: but when I visited his grave the path to it was still kept clear by the voluntary and indeed loving labour of the Samoans. Nor was this a light task, in that forest which was overrun by the mile-a-minute creeper. Every tree-trunk was smothered in it, and long festoons hung from every branch: so dense a curtain that no ray of the sun could ever pierce them. That deep respect which the Samoan felt for Stevenson gives him the right, I feel, to despise those other whites who do not live up to what *he knows* that a white man can be.

*　　*　　*

Do not imagine for a moment that all the whites

I met in Apia were of the same quality as my drunken planter, or the lachrymose beachcomber. This was far from the case. I met as much kindness in Apia from white men as from brown, and there were many names which I felt honoured to add to the roll of my friendship. There was a certain Mr. Rutherford, for instance, the Director of Education, who took me one day to see his schools. In these schools, apparently, segregation does not follow exactly the colour-line : aristocratic natives are classed with whites, and the lower-class natives classed by themselves. This seems a reasonable system where a better understanding between the white and the upper native classes is so desirable, but where to group either with the more backward class of natives would only render the whole attempt ridiculous.

Many of the natives come from distant villages, and are boarded at the school in native fashion. No attempt is made to overteach those who obviously will return to a rural life. A little reading, writing, and arithmetic, perhaps, with some history and geography, are their only bookish subjects. For the rest they are instructed chiefly in hygiene, and in the cultivation of native crops, so that on their return to their villages their influence may be of value to their fellows instead (as would have been the case if they had been crammed with purely bookish subjects) of being merely an irritation to them.

*   *   *

Leofa might ignore the half-castes, but I did not find it so easy—some of them were far too lovely. One of them—Eda—a dark-eyed, dark-haired school-girl of sixteen, quite stole my heart away.   We met casually, and I was enslaved before I quite knew what was happening.

It was time, I realized, that the sailor should go down again to the sea.

Five weeks I had spent at Apia, and now I must push on !   But it was a sad wrench.   The day I left, Eda and two other girls came to see me off. She was unusually shy, almost seemed inclined to run away ; but when my preparations for departure proved too long and tedious for the others, so that they wandered away down the jetty, it was Eda who remained behind.   At last, as I was preparing to cast off, she sang me in a sweet voice that well-known Samoan farewell song :

> " Lofa lau pele
>   Ole a su tea,
>   Ne nalo mai Apia
>   Seo ta Aiga," *etc.*

PART II

(" Good-bye, my darling
You are leaving now,
Do not forget Apia
And our comradeship," *etc.*)

Had I but shaved that morning I should never
have left Samoa. For had I shaved that morning
nothing would have prevented me from asking
Eda for a kiss ; and then the fat would have been
in the fire. I should have opened the bung-hole
of *Elaine* and sunk her to the bottom of the harbour.
In vain my aged parents would have waited my
return to Latvia.

But I had *not* shaved ; and so that kiss remained
unasked for. But never had the anchor I weighed
seemed so heavy, or the cheers of the onlookers as
I put to sea sounded more like a funeral dirge to
me.

CHAPTER XII

*June 25th : Danger Islands—A Tiny Community—Seventh
Day Adventism—Laxity of Morals—Communal Economy—
A Malthusian Riddle—A Melancholy Impression—A Long
Passage Ahead—Telling the Time by Jarvis Island—
Navigating by the Flight of Birds—A Curious Dream
—Logarithms for Breakfast—Waterspouts—I Fall Ill—
August 14th : Approaching Christmas Island*

SAMOA sank below the horizon, and I was on my
way to the Danger Islands.

I had a fair wind for once, the South-easterly
Trade. It was easy sailing, therefore. But navigation was becoming not so easy. I had only one
watch now, and had put a new spring in it in Suva.
But it was getting very erratic, and I did not feel at
all sure of the time. This meant that I could not
be sure of my longitude.

When you are not sure of your longitude, the
thing to do is to sail north or south till you get on
the latitude of your objective (since you can ascertain your latitude without knowing the exact time),
and then sail along that latitude until you run into
it. That method is all very well ; but for a single-
handed sailor, like myself, to run straight towards a

129

coral island surrounded by reefs without knowing how far off it is holds many dangers. I might pass close to it while asleep, and never see it at all : or equally I might run into it, head on, during the hours of darkness.

So I spent a good deal of time up the mast, my eyes skinned, and was lucky enough to sight some palm-trees over the horizon just after sunrise on the morning of 25th June. They appeared to be about eight miles away : and a couple of hours later I could make out the islands plainly.

There appeared to be a large triangular reef with a lagoon inside, and with a palm-grown island at each corner. The smallest of the three islands was the nearest to me ; and as I approached it I noticed a string of natives running along the shore. Presently a canoe came off with three men in it, who guided me to the anchorage. " The harbour," they called it. It was really only a dent in the outer reef on the lee side of the island : only safe for as long as the wind did not change.

They anchored me to the reef, and took me ashore. Two of them spoke fairly good English ; and I found that this island was normally uninhabited—the natives on it were there temporarily only, to gather copra. Their villages were on the other two islands : and on the biggest island of all there was a store in charge of a white man.

They told me that they had mistaken my boat for another one they were expecting, and so word had been sent to the Government Resident, who would be along presently.

Presently, indeed, the Government Resident arrived. He was an educated native, by the name of Geoffrey Henry. He seemed much surprised at my visit, and at the size of my boat : he made me welcome, and asked me to stay at his house on the main island. So I hoisted sail and with a couple of pilots sailed round the archipelago to its capital city. The harbour there, however, proved to be no better than the first one. High on the reef was the wreck of a three-hundred-ton schooner. She had called here to trade, I learned, and while the Captain was on shore a squall had come up and thrown her bodily like this right up on to the reef.

The same thing, I was afraid, might happen to my boat too ; so I asked Mr. Henry if there was some way of getting it into the lagoon. There was a shallow runway over the reef at a point near the main island, and so, when high tide came, with the help of one or two natives I dragged it over into the lagoon. This was not a very easy job, as only a few natives would help, the rest looking on with some disapproval.

Mr. Henry apologized for this : it was Sunday,

131

F

and his subjects were far too religious to do a hand's turn of work on that day of rest.

How was it then, I asked, that *any* of them had been willing to help me at all?

He explained that—small as the Danger Islands were—they contained three varieties of Christians. There were Protestants, Catholics and Seventh-Day-Adventists, each with their own missionaries. It was the Seventh-Day-Adventists of course, whose Sabbath falls on Saturday, who had felt no scruples about helping me on a Sunday!

So there are some conveniences after all, I reflected, in Seventh-Day-Adventism!

But truly these unhappy schisms between creeds do much harm to the good name of Christianity among the natives, and one should do everything possible to reduce their effect. Now the schism between the Seventh-Day-Adventists and those who held their Sabbath on Sunday might easily be cured, at a comparatively moderate expense. You remember what I told you about the date-line? How, if you are travelling east-about round the world, you gain an extra day in the year, and if you are travelling west-about you lose one?—What could be simpler than to ship all the Seventh-Day-Adventists in the South Seas in some senescent liner, and pack them off on the round trip, west-about? Every seventh day they would hold their sabbath:

but when they got home again, lo, a miracle would have occurred! Their seventh day would now be the Sunday of their fellow-Christians, and all would once more be sheep in a single fold!

Mr. Henry had many duties that do not fall to the ordinary lot of a governor. He was school-teacher, hydrographer, post-master, magistrate, harbour-master, customs officer, registrar, health officer—and probably a lot else. Of full native blood, he had studied in New Zealand, and as a young man had been a schoolmaster; but for the last eight years he had held his present post—or rather, multiplication of posts.

I have described the main outline of his little kingdom. The islands, of course, are entirely coral: there is no trace of any other rock in their composition. Consequently they are very flat: the highest point in the whole archipelago stands five feet above sea-level, and I wondered that they did not often get completely washed out in some big storm.

I learned, however, that this has only happened once within living memory. In 1914 a huge tidal wave did pass right over the islands. The trees survived: and indeed the Pandanus palm is seldom uprooted, even by the fiercest hurricane; for as it grows larger, certain shoots appear high up the trunk which grow in a downward direction until they take root in the ground, and hold the trunk firm like the guys of a flag-post. The natives, I take it, must have roosted in them ; for apparently no life was lost in the inundation. But in the aftermath of the inundation many lives were lost ; for the drinking-water was contaminated, and enteric fever broke out.

Joining island to island is the coral reef. It dries at low tide, and is as level as a table, but littered with coral boulders—some of which are the size of a motor-car—thrown up on it by gales ; and it is covered with patches of coral shingle, sea-shells, and coral sand.

The islands are covered with a dense growth of coconut and Pandanus palms : and though there cannot be more than five square miles of land in the whole group, they somehow support a population of six hundred souls. Life for the natives, however, is not here so rich as in a large island like Samoa : for very little that is edible, except coconut palms, will grow on the salty coral sand. There are just a few bananas and papayas, and in a tiny patch of swampy ground they grow some taro. Apart from this, of course, their natural staple is fish, and the greater part of their time, both day and night, is spent in fishing and spearing fish.

The diet seems to suit them, however, for they are a healthy and contented lot, with that fine set

134

By courtesy " B. M."

The camping-hut
The Pandanus palm

[134]

of teeth which you will find anywhere among a
population living on a diet composed almost entirely
of a single article—whether it is the fruit-eating
Polynesian, or the meat-eating Eskimo.

Before Christianity in its three forms took a hold
in the islands, the morals of these natives I am told
used to be terribly lax. The women would not
refuse any man, and even children could be seen
misconducting themselves in public. There were
no official marriages, and by mutual consent the
children from birth were allotted to one or other of
the parents, and to his or her family. Sanitary
conditions too were deplorable. Each family had
their burying ground—generally just outside their
hut. Without question, the advent of white man's
rule has been beneficent for these islands. Sanita-
tion and morals have alike been improved. Under
the influence of religion marriages are encouraged,
and a divorce cannot be had without payment of a
fee of fifteen-shillings (this does not sound much,
but it means several months' wages for a native,
and that gives him time to think the matter over
if it is just some petty quarrel).

The economics of the islands are fairly simple.
The taro patch is divided up in the proportion of
three square yards to every soul : and every man,
woman, or child who has such a patch must either
cultivate it or have it cultivated for him by the

working members of the family. The coconut crop, on the other hand, which is entirely wild, belongs to the whole community. Everyone picks what he likes for himself, but unconsumed nuts are turned into copra, and sold ; and the proceeds divided amongst the whole population, each man and woman receiving a share, and each child a half-share.

The labour in this communal industry is, of course, general, and given without direct wages. Methods too are primitive, and consequently in every department of life much labour is needed to procure small results. Timber being scarce, all timber work—whether it be a canoe or the parish church—is built of small bits and pieces dexterously tied together with " sennit," a kind of plaited rope made from the fibre of the coconut husk.

Now the swampy patch suitable for growing taro (you will remember) is limited in size ; and yet each member of the population is allotted a fixed area of it. What happens, you will wonder as I did, when the population increases ?

The odd thing is that the population does not increase. It has remained stationary for time out of mind. I questioned Mr. Henry closely on this point. Malthus could give no answer : because if the islands were able to export two hundred and forty tons of copra per annum, there was no reason in the Malthusian theory why they should not increase their numbers until they ate that copra themselves—an increase in the population to four times their present numbers. And the sea, of course, could give them as many fish as there were fishermen to catch it. Nor was it due to tribal wars : they had not been involved in any war for fully a hundred years. Nor were they depressed, melancholy, suicidal : they were as cheerful and industrious a lot as you would find anywhere.

Mr. Henry made several physiological suggestions, none of which would hold water ; and none of which I think did he really believe in himself. For the truth of the matter of course is that the limitation of population is voluntary—Polynesian women are past mistresses in the arts of contraception. Why do they do it ? I suppose it is in order to keep up their standard of living ; for they are, of course, dependent for whatever they import on the receipts from that two hundred and forty tons of copra that they export. If the population increases, not only would the money have to be divided into smaller shares, but there would be less copra to export, and so less money to divide. I do not myself think that we shall see any great change in the population of the Danger Islands until or unless more scientific industrial techniques are introduced : or unless the tariff system, which here as elsewhere bleeds trade white, is seriously modified.

PART II

Nor is it only the extortions of the government from which the producer of copra suffers : the white trader is not always so honest as he should be. There was a schooner which called at these islands some years ago to trade. The natives carried all their available copra down to the beach. The captain loaded it, and called the elders aboard. In payment for the copra he gave them a roll of dungaree cloth, a roll of calico print, a box of fish-hooks, and a bagful of money. Then he hurried them ashore, and hoisted anchor.

At first the natives were overjoyed with the payment : for these articles were the very things they needed. But their joy was clouded when they opened the bag of money, and found it contained nothing but copper—no silver and gold, as they had expected. So they went to the Government Resident, and complained of having been cheated.

The problem was not an easy one for him, as the natives had not the slightest idea how much copra they had sold. They could only say it was " a big lot."

" Did you not get it weighed ? " he asked them.

" Oh, yes," said they, " the Captain weighed it."

" Well, what was the weight ? "

" We don't know : he did not tell us."

" Then perhaps this payment is all you are really entitled to ? "

138

" No, no," they said ; " this payment is little : we sold a *big* lot of copra ! "

So the matter had to remain, for the time being : but when that schooner called again the Resident impounded her books, and saw by them that the copra taken on board that time had been eighty tons. At this rate the payment was only a fraction of the minimum payment fixed by the Government ; and so the Captain was now forced to pay up in full.

Taking it all in all, this island left a melancholy impression upon me : I cannot say why. I suppose the community was too small : the isolation too complete : life was stagnant there. An ocean graveyard, in which men were born and lived among the graves. After eleven days I pushed on once more : and as I left the islands the last thing I heard was the melancholy crying of a bereaved father.

Some time before, his beloved wife had left him. Before the white man came he could have waylaid his rival, and won back his wife by force of arms : but now he had no remedy except impotent tears, and the company of his only child, a youngster of nine years old. Just before I landed this youngster had fallen from a palm tree, and hurt himself mortally. Now, three weeks after the accident, he had died.

Those mournful cries were the last thing I heard of Danger Islands, as on the morning of the 7th July I put out once more to sea.

*   *   *

I had now a long run ahead of me : a thousand miles of ocean to cross before I should come to Christmas Island.

Towards the end of that thousand-mile run I should cross the Equator.

I spun along merrily with the south-east Trades for the first week : but as I drew near the Line I had my first real experience of the doldrums— nothing but rain-squalls and intermittent calms, no steady sailing weather at all. These squalls kept me eternally on the *qui vive*, as I had to be ready at any moment to reef the jib. Consequently I did what I ought to have done before : I rigged a jib in-haul. Up till now I had gone out on the bowsprit whenever the jib needed reefing : but this is a dangerous practice, with the bowsprit plunging like a bucking horse, and no one at the helm to go back for you if you happen to take a toss into the sea.

The eternal damp, too, gave the *coup de grâce* to the two cheap watches I had to serve me as chrono- meters : they became more and more erratic, and I could no longer trust them. So I sailed north until I found myself on the latitude of Jarvis Island (just south of the Equator), and then decided to run east ; so as to sight that island and get the right time there.

That does not mean that I should go ashore and ask an inhabitant to look at his watch for me : for one thing, Jarvis Island has no inhabitants. And yet you can tell the time by it just as accurately as if it had ; for Jarvis Island—any island—has a fixed longitude, which you can read from the chart. When you find yourself in sight of such an island, and bearing directly north or south from it—why, then you know your own longitude too. And just as you can calculate your own longitude if you know the Greenwich time, so you can calculate the Greenwich time if you know your longitude. In either case it is just a matter of taking sights, and working out calculations.

So I turned my course to the east—on the latitude of Jarvis Island, and with about a couple of hundred miles to go in that direction—and sailed along its parallel in order to find it.

I have already told you of the dangers inherent in sailing plumb towards an island, when you do not know how far off it may be. But there are certain things which mitigate those dangers. I was learning to read other signs than those of lunar and solar altitudes—the signs of the sea itself, and of the sky.

Like the ancient Greeks and Romans I took my
omens by birds. I did not know my longitude : but
none the less I knew each day that I was drawing
nearer to Jarvis. I could tell this by the ever-
increasing number of sea-birds. Just before sunset
I would see them flying home to the eastward :
big mobs of them : mixed lots of boobies and terns,
sometimes, or sometimes flocks of one kind only.

When they noticed my boat they would generally
swerve from their course to examine it. The terns
were the more inquisitive and talkative. They
would swoop to have a good look, and then off they
would go again : and then, as they went, they would
turn back once more to have just another look at
it ; and to express their opinion in notes of surprise,
derision, or warning.

All the same, it was the boobies I found the more
dependable guides. Flocks of them would fly, low,
straight as an arrow, for their destination. They
were not so easily distracted from their purpose as
the terns, and seldom expressed an opinion.

One night, however, the boobies behaved dif-
ferently. A flock of fully a thousand of them came
past my boat. But this time they did not neglect
it. Every one of that huge mob turned aside,
circled once round my mast before he went on
again. In that brief little moment of circling, each
keen eye took in the smallest detail like the lens of

a camera. I will frankly confess that I felt more flattered by the attention of these birds than the stares of idlers on the beaches at Suva and Apia.

It was a long time since I had any experiences of what might be described as a spiritual nature, such as the voice and the dreams of the earlier part of my voyage. But now, after I had been for several weeks at sea, something of the same sort occurred again. I dreamed one night that I was floating in the air above the dark ocean : and I knew myself to be roughly a hundred miles to the N.N.E. of my boat's present position. There on the ocean, on the dark water below me, I saw a curious hull, which I took to be a derelict. As I looked at it the light increased, and I made it out to be a ship with a stumpy mast ; and the Captain's bridge aft, resembling a hen-coop.

I woke up, and remembering my experience with the dream of the lighthouse I skinned my eyes for fear I might be about to run into something. But I could see nothing in the murky darkness, so I turned in again ; for after all, if the dream was true, was not the derelict I had sighted some hundred miles away ?

The next morning, as I took my first peep outside my berth, I saw about a mile ahead the very duplicate of the ship I had dreamed about. She looked like a steamer, but there was no smoke coming from her stack. I wondered if she was in fact a derelict. But, no : she was moving : she crossed my course in a southerly direction. It was not till I drew closer that I was able to make her out to be a diesel-engined freighter, with a deck-cargo of timber, bound for Samoa or New Zealand. I passed her within half a mile : but I doubt if she noticed me.

This dream was in its way just as remarkable as the one about the lighthouse : for never since that once had I dreamed again about sailing or the sea : never at all had I dreamed about a ship : and never till that moment had I passed a ship of any kind on the high seas. In some ways indeed it was the more remarkable dream of the two. For the lighthouse dream might have been prompted by the imminence of danger : I was really close to the reef and lighthouse when I dreamed about them. But at the time I dreamed of this steamer she was far below the horizon, and it was not till the next day that our paths crossed.

If dreams like this mean that the soul wanders from the body, it is a curious fact that the soul nevertheless remains clearly conscious of just where the body is at the time. I told you that in this dream of the steamer I knew that I had left my body behind a hundred miles to the S.S.W. The next night I had another dream of the same kind.

144

This time I was floating in the air about half a mile above the surface of the sea, at a point about fifty miles east of my boat and five miles south of it. Looking to the south from my vantage point, I could see as clearly as by day a small coral island, oval in shape, with an under-water reef projecting from it in a north-easterly direction. There was some stunted growth on the island. The sea-ripple seemed wonderfully realistic : and I could see rollers breaking heavily on the eastern side : round the reef itself there was comparative calm, and a landing might have been effected on either side of it.

That island I never saw. I have no means of knowing whether it resembles Jarvis Island or not ; for I never saw Jarvis Island. Perhaps some other seafarer, who reads this passage, will some day be able to enlighten me.

The dream, however, left me positive that I was getting close to the island : and that it lay at about the distance and direction I had dreamed. Being so close, I had to be on guard lest I run into it in the night.

But squally weather had set in now, alternating with calms, which made progress difficult for a sailing-boat : and the situation was further complicated by the powerful ocean currents which wash back and forth across the Equator. As I was ignor-

ant of my longitude and dependent for knowledge
of my latitude on noon sights of the sun, and the
sun was at that time so often hidden in a rain-
squall ; and since I could not sail by dead-reckoning
because I did not know the force and direction of the
currents, it was exceedingly difficult for me to be
at all certain of finding Jarvis.

The only indication upon which I could depend
with any reliance was the evening flights of the sea-
birds ; and on the evening of 1st July, after a
day of fierce sailing through heavy squalls, I
observed that these birds no longer flew eastward,
but were wending their way home to the south-west.
Plainly, therefore, I had passed Jarvis.

Just before sunset, however, through a rift in
a bank of mist, I saw what might have been land
lying some four miles to the south-west.

If that was land I did not want to charge into
it in the darkness : so I lowered the mainsail and
trusted to the slight easterly drift to carry me close
within sight of it by dawn.

When dawn came, however, there was no land
to be seen. The breeze had died away : a glassy
calm had followed : thousands of Portuguese Men-
of-War (nautili)—those curious jelly-fish which put
to sea with a jelly sail—were floating on the
unruffled surface of the sea. Deep in the clear
water a multitude of fishes could be seen : and

flocks of sea-birds were feeding on the small fry which their submarine enemies had driven to the surface.

My sail was useless, and unknown currents were carrying me I knew not whither. But I was lucky enough to get a noon sight of the sun that day, and I then found myself to be some twenty miles north of the latitude of Jarvis.

For the next two days the same sort of weather continued : I was at the mercy of cross-currents in the sea, and fitful squalls and calms in the air : and I could not tell whether I was being carried back towards Jarvis, or washed farther from the island.

So when at last a steady south-easterly breeze set in, I decided to take the hint and waste no more time over that elusive island but sail on for Christmas Island—which is much bigger, and thus less easily missed like this.

My uncertainty about longitude, however, was now even more serious. Christmas Island lay somewhere to the north : but was I to the east or the west of it ? It was absolutely essential that I should find out : for otherwise I should in all probability sail past Christmas Island—out into the empty wastes of the northern Pacific.

The old navigation book which I had on board told me that when other methods fail it is possible

to tell the time at sea by observations of the moon—
or rather, by observations of the distance between
the sun and moon. It looked a difficult piece of
headwork : but it was my only chance. Luckily
one of those evenings, while I was becalmed near
Jarvis, I managed to obtain two nearly equal altitude sights of the sun and moon—one west and the
other east. All the next day, therefore, I was
busy with my calculations. Great exactitude was
necessary : seconds of time, which (owing to the
nature of my chronometers) I was in the habit of
omitting in my ordinary longitude calculations, had
now to be taken into exact account. The whole day
from dawn to dusk was a procession of logarithms
—logarithms for breakfast, lunch and dinner.

But at last I completed my reckoning. I then
had Greenwich time within an error of no more
than a few minutes : and it confirmed my belief
that I must have been very close to Jarvis on that
night of July 31st.

But, more important still, I was now able to
shape my course for Christmas Island with reasonable confidence.

To take advantage of the currents and Trade
Winds, I decided to approach Christmas Island from
the east. I was not the first to make that mistake
—fourteen shipwrecks on the island's eastern shore
bear witness of it (however, of that more anon).

I Fall Ill

I was now on the Equator, and I sailed east along the Line until the flight of sea-birds told me that I had passed the island. Then I cut up north, and back along the second parallel.

Now two new dangers made their appearance. A number of waterspouts could be seen on various parts of the horizon, like trunks of an aqueous forest, in which I was fearful that my boat might be overwhelmed. But luckily none ever came near enough to do me damage. The other danger was on board with me. Some rice or fish that had been left over from the previous day, and which I had re-heated, poisoned me so badly that for two days I could hardly get in or out of my bunk. Those two days, of course, the boat had to take care of herself.

On the third morning I woke to hear something breathing alongside my boat. On struggling to look out I saw three large black porpoises, big as the boat, keeping me company a few yards off. Following their peculiar habit, they would swim in formation, plunging in and out of the water in complete accord : and every time their heads appeared above the surface you heard that regular breathing.

But of course my boat was too slow a companion for them ; and presently they cut away to one side. But a few minutes later I saw one of them standing up perpendicularly like a post out of the water, as if he were looking for me.

You remember the shoal of fish that travelled with me between Fiji and Samoa ? There was a school of little fish now that followed me as faithfully as the Pillar of Fire and Smoke that led the Hebrews in the desert : by night they were phosphorescent streaks under my boat, and by day I could see them so clearly that I came to know them, fish from fish, by old scars or peculiar markings on their bodies. They kept close company with me : if I forged ahead, they forged ahead : if I tacked, they tacked with me. But I was now getting very near to Christmas Island : and once more the fear of running into land at night kept me awake. Birds were becoming more plentiful, and now, even before daylight, I could hear the occasional squawk of passing terns setting out for their feeding grounds.

Then, on the morning of the 14th August, at sunrise, I saw big mobs of sea-birds feeding all round.

I was just beginning to wonder if the currents had carried me past the island to the north or south, when I sighted a flight of boobies. They held their steady course right from the direction in which I was headed, so revealing to me unmistakably that Christmas Island still lay in front.

Sure enough, a few hours later the tops of a few scrubby trees appeared above the water.

Jostled by Sharks—Currents—A Charming French Planter—Half a Million Coconut Palms—A Plague of Black Cats—Dogs that Catch Sharks—Mutton-birds—I Make Myself a Passport—M. Rougier Visas it—August 25th : to Sea Again—The Doldrums—Squalls—The N.E. Trades at Last—The Booby and the Frigate-bird—September 15th : Hawaii Sighted—Arrival at Honolulu

SOON I could discern the low sandy shore, and within three-quarters of an hour I was close to the mighty rollers that were speeding towards the beach. I could feel the ground swell already. As the entrance to the lagoon is on the north-west side, I decided to round the island along the north shore. But no sooner had I set my course than something unexpected happened. Of a sudden the sea around me was aboil with sharks—hundreds of them. They were squirming round and under the boat, and were bumping it with sledge-hammer blows. The water their tails splashed up fell into the boat in showers.

Had they mistaken my boat for a strange sea-beast ? Or were they bent on the devilish purpose of smashing it, as a blackbird smashes

a snail, in the hope of getting the morsel—me—
within ?

I felt the boat could not stand the banging for
long : she seemed to be leaking already . . . So
this was to be my end ? To be eaten by sharks off
Christmas Island, and not a soul to know what had
become of me !

Should I run on to the reef ? The sharks would
hardly follow me into the breakers. There was
a chance in that case of my reaching the shore
alive, even if my boat got capsized and smashed.

No, I decided, I will keep to the open and fight it
out. So I took my spear and began to prod left and
right. The spear-point soon bent. I straightened
it several times, but each time it grew weaker.
So I took a jack-knife, and tied it to the spear-
handle. This will give them a tidy jab, I thought.

But I had no need to use it. As suddenly as the
sharks had come they disappeared. It was only
then it dawned on me what they really wanted.
That was neither me nor my boat : it was the
school of faithful little fish that had been accom-
panying me for weeks, and probably looked to me
for protection.

Most of them were now gone. About a hundred
were still left, however, hanging close round the stern
of the boat. The mob of sharks were gone too ;
but now a dozen Tuna-fish were following me. A

hungry lot ! A chip of wood I tossed overboard was swallowed instantly.

Did one of the remaining little fish lag behind even for an instant, there would be a flash as the Tuna darted past and the little fish would be no more.

All day long I sailed along the northern shore of Christmas Island. Night was coming on, and still I had not rounded the western point. The breeze had died away, but I could see by watching the shore-line creeping past the stars that a three-knot current was carrying me along still.

What should I do ? If I went to sleep and allowed the boat to drift, by morning Christmas Island would be out of sight : and it was impossible to tell how long I might have to wait for breeze enough to work back against that current.

" No," I said to myself, " this is not going to be Jarvis Island over again."

So, though I had had hardly any sleep the two previous nights, I made up my mind to stay up all night if necessary, and to steer my boat till I succeeded in working her into the lee of the island.

With the faintest of draughts, inch by inch I took her out of the current. By midnight I had rounded the western point, and the morning sun found me at the lagoon entrance.

Barely had I managed to scrape off a month's growth of whiskers when I saw a motor-launch approaching. It contained several natives and the manager of the island—a M. Paul Rougier, a tall distinguished-looking Frenchman with a Van Dyck beard. He asked me in perfect English what had brought me there : then shook hands, and said that when first he saw my boat he took me for a ship-wrecked mariner. Then he gave me a tow to the jetty inside the lagoon. I tied up to the jetty by the head, and threw the anchor out astern. To my surprise—and the great merriment of the natives —the anchor-rope snapped in two. A native diver retied it to the anchor again, but the moment a strain came on it, it snapped again. It was a three-inch rope of coconut fibre which I had bought second-hand in Sydney. It was strong enough then ; but constant exposure on the deck of my boat had rotted it. So I had now to use some light hemp as a warp. and, having made fast, I stepped ashore.

By now I had become so hardened a navigator that the land no longer rocked, but seemed quite steady under my feet. M. Rougier told me that the whole island (which is a large one, forty miles by twenty) belonged to a copra company : that he, his wife and his baby were the only white inhabitants on it. In addition there were about a hundred

Tahitian natives, imported there under contract as labourers.

He introduced me to his wife and to his son, who was a few months old.

I asked Madame Rougier if she did not feel lonely, so far away from the world. She said she did not ; and M. Rougier also seemed perfectly happy.

" Time was," he said, " that I did not like babies. Now I do not know how on earth I should get on without this one."

This was no idle boast, for he spent hours with it : and by the affection he displayed towards his wife I doubt if a happier couple could be found any-where on the face of the earth. Towards me, moreover, they showed themselves uncommonly hospitable. They put me up in the vacant sub-manager's cottage ; and for the first time in my voyage I had a good bed to sleep on.

Moreover, I enjoyed the real French cooking.

Every three months, M. Rougier told me, the company's schooner from Tahiti called for a cargo of copra : but in the meantime he was sole monarch, and solely responsible for everything that happened on the island. Like the captain of a ship he had to be prepared for every emergency : for sickness and for accident. Like a ship's crew, moreover, the labourers under him were not native to the island, but imported on a two-years' contract—a contract which combined the wage and the piecework systems.

Business was humming. M. Rougier's company was profiting, it seemed, by its French nationality. For though, with the slump, the price of copra had fallen in world markets, the value of the franc had fallen even lower. Expressed in francs, therefore, the price had actually risen ; and business was brisk with them. They had more than half a million trees on the island : which should—by the time this book is through the press—be producing six thousand tons of copra every year !

Christmas Island, of course, is a coral island : a ring or horseshoe of low land surrounding a central lagoon which teems with fish (and sharks). At first sight a coral island looks very uninviting : the rough shingle, the glaring sand, the sparse vegetation. And it would be more than uninviting, it would be impossible to inhabit were it not for the coconut palm. It is this blessed tree which supplies shade, food, drink, housing and revenue. Amongst coral islands, Christmas Island has many advantages. Although almost on the Equator its climate is not over hot, but one of the most equable on the earth : and it is remarkably free from pests : there are no mosquitoes, no flies ; no snakes, termites, elephant beetles or poisonous plants.

There is only one notable pest, and that is the wild cat.

These cats are black. Doubtless they are the progeny of some ships' mascots, who survived the wrecks piled on the eastern reef. They have played havoc with the smaller bird life—and will attack fowls, it you keep any. As a defence against them M. Rougier keeps almost a small pack of fox terriers. They are very effective in destroying the cats ; but he has to take the utmost care that they too do not run wild in their turn : for then he would have to import leopards to keep down the dogs !

The fox terrier is an adaptable animal. These would even swim out into the lagoon and fetch little sharks ashore.

Nor were the sharks in the lagoon by any means merely a nuisance. The labourers would kill them if they got a chance, with a blow of a stone : then they hauled them ashore, and cut off the fins. These latter they dried in the sun : and afterwards they were exported to China, where they are considered a delicacy. There are other uses to which a shark can be put : an oil like cod-liver oil can be extracted from him, and his skin makes fine shagreen leather. But at present only the fins of those caught at Christmas Island are put to a commercial purpose.

* * *

One day M. Rougier took me to one of what he called the " bird islands " in the lagoon. The wild cats could not reach it : and young mutton-birds were so plentiful, in shallow holes in the ground, that you had to be careful not to step on them. They are about the size of a chicken, and one of the fattest birds living. Freshly roasted they are far from despicable.

I had eaten stewed mutton-birds in Australia, so I told M. Rougier that I would like to take a few with me, salted. He immediately ordered a couple of native boys to get a hundred of them for me : and all next day they were busy skinning and pickling them. I also told him how much I fancied that coconut sauce which I have described : so straightway he set a couple of boys to the task of grating up undried copra, and squeezing the cream out of it for me. In fact, he could not in any way have shown himself kinder. He had my boat hauled up and repainted for me. He offered me a new suit of sails : and he even offered me an out-board motor, but this I refused on principle, for I had come so far without a motor that I was deter-mined to complete my journey without one. But he insisted on my taking a supply of tinned foods with me, and onions, yams and coconuts. I had never yet met such generosity in any man, and it almost made me blush to accept all the favours that

158

were showered on me. I had no idea how wealthy in fact these people were : it was not till a year later that I learned that M. Rougier had been left an estate worth millions.

When M. Rougier heard that I was travelling without a passport he told me that I was sure to strike trouble when I tried to land in the States.

" You will find plenty of nice people there," he told me, " but their administration is at least a thousand years behind the times."

He told me how, a year ago, he had been bound for Europe. The shortest route, of course, lay across the States : and so the Company's schooner took him to Los Angeles. Now his passport had been issued at Tahiti : and Tahiti is about one thousand five hundred miles south of Christmas Island. So, because he had not made the round trip of three thousand miles to Tahiti and back to collect a visa from the American consul there— no other American consul would do—the Immigration Authorities were unwilling to let him land !

So now I knew what I could expect myself. It was plainly necessary that I should have a passport.

But why should I apply to any Government for one ? I ruled my own life : no Government ruled me. I had made my own sextant and other necessities for the voyage : why should I not issue my own passport ? So that is what I proceeded to do ;

and without charging myself any fee drew up the document you will see on the opposite page.

I was not prepared, however, to sail back to Suva in order to have this document *visé* by the American Consul there—even if he had been willing to attach his visa to such an unusual document. I would sail on, and take my chance. But since one visa might be expected to attract others—like sheep going through a gap in a hedge—I started my collection with the only visa there available— that of M. Paul Rougier, as representing the Government of Christmas Island.

So, on the morning of 25th August, I took my departure from Christmas Island. I had now another long run ahead of me—the twelve-hun- dred-mile run to Honolulu. I half thought of calling at Fanning Island on the way—it is only about one hundred and fifty miles north-west from Christmas Island. But corrosion had put my taf- frail-log altogether out of commission, and, between my " fixes " by the sun, I had no way of checking the distance run. Moreover, I was being borne northward by a strong current, and I soon found that I had been carried past that island.

Then once more I was visited by a series of squalls —doldrum weather. Tropical squalls are very try- ing. Usually they are preceded by a calm. The boat rocks, the sail flaps, the boom bashes about.

— PASSPORT —

The bearer of this passport
— Fred Rebell —
of no allegiance, is travelling
from Sydney, Australia, via
Pacific Ocean, United States of
America and Atlantic Ocean
to his native town Windau
in the country of Latvia.
Description of bearer:
Sex: male. Age: 46 years.
Height 5 ft. 8 in. Eyes: blue
Complexion: fair. —

Photograph
of bearer
F. Rebell

Dated this
3 march 1932
Signature: F Rebell

This passport has been vised at:

Christmas Island
Arrived.- 15/8/32
Dep 25/8/32
Elliot'

Honolulu Terros. Hawaii

Geo. F. Wright
Munpr Clk & Conty of Hm Rb
Cal. 7/8/32

Los Angeles California U.S.A

home-made passport

To prevent chafe (both of the cordage and of your own nerves) you jump on deck, and lower away the main-sail. Then on one side of the horizon you notice a heavy dark cloud, ragged underneath, with one or more sheets of rain anchoring it, as it were, to the ocean. Slowly the squall approaches ; the swell gets bigger ; a few drops of rain fall, and a slight draught sets in. Thereupon you hoist the mainsail again and creep back under cover to await the squall. Will it, or will it not, be too fierce for your boat to carry sail ?

Presently the rain starts. There is tremendous force in a slanting sheet of rain : the boat heels over and bounds wildly forward, and you watch anxiously, lest she run gunwale-under and you have to nip out and get the sail down again. For occasions like these I rigged a trip-line, by pulling at which I could let the jib halyards go. Thereupon the jib would flop down, the boat would round up to the squall, and stop.

You have to keep your eye on tiller and compass also ; for very often a squall starts blowing from one direction and finishes up from another : so you find yourself travelling off your course.

Not every squall hits you, naturally : and sometimes you get fooled. First comes the calm, then the slight blow : you hoist sail, expecting the whole rigmarole : but the breeze falls again, and the sail slats about till you can stand it no longer and are driven to take it in. The squall has passed you by in another direction.

In this squally weather it would have been very difficult to put back to Fanning Island : nor was there much reason to do so. Except for a cable station, it is only just such another plantation as Christmas Island, but smaller. Moreover, I had a hunch that this unusual south-westerly draught was soon bound to give way to a strong easterly. If I was ready to make use of that easterly when it came, it would soon see me out of the doldrums.

My surmise proved correct : the wind gradually backed round to south-east, and for a couple of days it blew so hard that I had to take in the mainsail and run under jib only. Other sailing vessels have been hung up in the doldrums for weeks : I was very lucky to get through in record time.

I don't like the doldrums. I was more than glad to be out of the Equatorial regions, and in the steady north-easterly Trades, which promised me a good run right up to Hawaii.

Trade-wind sailing is easy sailing : you have little to do in the way of managing your ship. In the daytime I amused myself by watching the different birds feeding. The booby, for instance, would spot his prey under the surface, then fold his wings and drop into the sea like a stone. He never missed. In a second or two he is up again on the surface : you do not see the fish, only a big bulge travelling down his neck . . . and usually he finishes his meal with a drink of salt-water.

Some seafarers assert that the booby does not catch whole fish, but instead bites chunks out of the backs of big ones. I made every effort to determine whether this is true, but I could never be sure.

Then there is the frigate-bird. Eagle-like, he spends most of his time soaring high overhead : and he gets his meal in a different manner. He watches for flying-fish : as they leave the water he swoops down, catches them in mid-air and soars up again. But the flying-fish, thus caught, is not easy to swallow. Caught by the tail or the middle he keeps his wings open : therefore the frigate bird throws him from his beak and catches him once more—by the head this time—and so swallows him down.

My taffrail-log was now useless : I could no longer rely on my watches : but neither of these things caused me much worry. The Sandwich Islands are large, and there was little likelihood of my missing them. My course was now due north : with a fair wind, I could keep to it pretty accurately : and noon altitudes of the sun, by giving me my latitude, gave me also exactly the progress I was making.

I had by now acquired a contemplative mind, and the three weeks of this passage passed quickly enough. Night after night the Southern Cross ever more closely hugged the horizon, and at last disappeared altogether as the Pole Star came into view. Once more the sky was lit by those familiar northern constellations that I had not seen for so many years.

It was on the morning of the 15th September that I sighted Hawaii, about forty miles to starboard. As I approached it, however, the high mountain completely choked the breeze ; and though there was a heavy swell coming round each end of the island, I had not a breath to steady me. For nearly a day my boat lay there, rocking most uncomfortably. When at last a blow did set in it carried me to Lanai, another of the Hawaian group. About twelve miles south of Lanai I again got becalmed —again on account of a mountain blocking the Trade Wind. Every now and then there would be a breath or two ; I would hoist sail and make a few miles' progress, only to find myself drifting back again in the ensuing calm. In desperation I tried rowing, but after an hour's exhausting work I seemed to be doing no good : so I gave it up as a bad job.

Then, as if to try my patience still further, one tiresome little harbinger of land flew out to meet me. It was a black stinging ant, and after the long aerial voyage it had accomplished—when you would have expected it to have little thought for anything but rest—what must it do, but set to work immediately on landing at crawling inside my shirt and stinging me all round the waist !

Gradually, however, I did make progress, a mile or two at a time. Oahu, the island Honolulu is on, was as yet below the horizon ; but now at night I could see the glow of the city lights on the clouds in the north-west.

At last, on the third day, a sharp blow set in, and within twenty-four hours I was just opposite Honolulu harbour, where I dropped anchor for the night.

Early next morning my yellow flag was up, and I watched till noon ; but nobody seemed to take any notice : so I raised anchor and sailed right in.

I had been twenty-six days on the way from Christmas Island : and because of the great number of drinking coconuts I had been supplied with my water consumption for this passage had amounted to only six gallons ! Less than a quart a day. I had still about thirty gallons of water in my tanks, and enough food for six months. Even if I had missed the Sandwich Islands, I still should have made the

American coast without much trouble : and I could hardly have missed *that*.

Luckily during the run my watch had kept a fairly even rate, so I was barely thirty miles out in my longitude reckoning.

CHAPTER XIV

*Description of Honolulu—My Home-made Passport—
Visiting the Island Sights—Youthful Imitators—A Discussion
on Religion—Navigation by Dream—A Comparison with
the Homing Instinct of Birds—November 3rd : Good-bye
to Honolulu—A Long Lap : A Three-thousand mile Passage
Ahead*

WITH the little yellow flag at the mast-head I
tacked up Honolulu Harbour. When I was abreast
of the Aloha Tower a motor-launch came after me.

" Where are you from ? " he hailed.

" Christmas Island and Sydney ! " I answered—
but the latter, of course, he could read from the
stern of my boat. He stared at me for a minute ;
and I guarantee I never saw such an astounded look
on any man's face.

" Well, you had better pull up at the quarantine
station," he said at last : " it is right opposite ;
we'll give you a tow if you want."

But I had no need of a tow, with the wind aft :
so I lowered the mainsail and drifted up under the
jib. Then I dropped anchor, and tied the stern of
my boat to the wall. " We have phoned the
doctor," said the same man : " he will be along

in a minute, with the Harbour-Master. What sort
of a trip have you had?"

" Fine."

" Care for some iced water?"

Presently the doctor arrived, and had a look at
my bills of health from Suva, Apia, and Christmas
Island. He said I should have had one from
Sydney too ; but all the same he wrote out a landing
permit. After all, there were few diseases which
could have lurked undetected in my carcass for
nearly twelve months.

Next came the Harbour-Master's launch, bringing me some letters. He kindly towed me to a
good berth at Pier 12.

There my boat lay for a week. Crowds used
to gather to have a look at my ship and to ply
me with questions. Newspaper reporters, photo-
graphers, and movie people kept coming on board.
It was not very nice to be stared at, but I was
compensated by invitations to lunch and to the
homes of various nice people.

Honolulu is much bigger than Suva, of course ;
but like Suva it is a cosmopolitan place. Instead
of Britishers most of the white people here are
American (it was amongst these latter I principally
moved), and instead of Indians, the Japanese pre-
dominate here. By their frugality and industry
they are capturing all trade.

One American friend I talked to, who had a large and adolescent family, was much concerned at the difficulty of placing his boys and girls with advantage. " The Japanese are everywhere here," he said. " They are multiplying like rabbits : they have families of ten or twelve and somehow educate them all. They work cheaper than the white man and are squeezing him out everywhere. If only the United States would take over the administration, and deal with the menace ! "

And yet I noticed that this patriotic gentleman would himself patronize Japanese shops : he did not disdain to utilize the cheaper Japanese service when it was to his personal profit : and I doubt if he even noticed the inconsistency in his attitude.

One sees very few pure-blooded natives, for they are more than twenty times outnumbered by the other races—by Japanese, Filipinos, Chinese, Portuguese, half-castes and Koreans. For those who remain, hopelessly impoverished, " Welcoming the visitor " has become the chief industry : " Lei "-making, hula-dancing and steel guitar music. But even in these lines of his own he has now to compete with other races ! Years ago, they say, the missionaries came to this island with nothing but the Bible. Now, the native has nothing but the Bible ! Or next to nothing ! It is true the Government still holds a little land reserved for the homeless native ; but it is mostly coral soil that will grow only coconuts. Sign-boards with the word " Kapu " (" prohibited ") written on them are conspicuous all over the island. Indeed, Kapu seems to be the one native word in everyday use. No wonder this expropriated race has shrunk to such a minority.

The second day I was in port, an officer from the Immigration Department asked me to call at his office.

The first thing he wanted to know was whether I had a passport.

" Sure," said I, and produced the one I had written out for myself—bearing as its only visa the official stamp of M. Rougier, affixed at Christmas Island.

Needless to say, this document rather flummoxed the Immigration officer. " This is not an *official* passport," he complained.

" What makes a passport official ? " I asked him.

" Well, it must be issued by a man's government," he said.

" I am my own government," I answered : " and I issued myself this passport, so it is official."

" Well, then," he said, " it has not got an American Visa."

" That is true," I answered. " Granted, I have omitted taking the trifling trouble of travelling

170

three thousand miles for the privilege of presenting an American Consul with ten dollars. I admit it. But the point is, what are you going to do about it? It is the only passport I have. If you will not accept it you have no alternative but to push me back into the sea."

This made him uncomfortable. "No," he said: "we won't do that."

It ended with their taking from me a statement long enough to make a three-volume biography: my nationality, pedigree, relations, education, occupation, previous residences, intentions—and what not. But they did not push me back into the sea.

A couple of days later a bill came from the quarantine station: five dollars, for doctor's fees. I was a bit disgruntled at this; for it was the first time I have ever heard of such a fee being charged to any single-handed sailor. A gentleman I complained to immediately pulled out a five-dollar bill, and offered it to me; but of course, I could not accept it like that. Later, however, a gathering of yachtsmen made up a collection, in small amounts, to pay my quarantine expenses; and that I could not very well refuse, without being churlish.

Honolulu looked prosperous enough, and the prices of things were higher than I had struck anywhere before. However, people told me those prices were nothing to what they used to be before the depression.

"O-ho," said I, "so you have the depression here? I hadn't noticed it."

"That is because you did not know Honolulu before," they answered. "Look at our tourist traffic! It has dwindled to nothing. Look at the slump in the pineapple-canning industry! The price of pines has fallen so low it doesn't pay to cart them to the cannery. Planters let them rot in the ground. The only industry which still keeps its head above water is the sugar industry; for the United States has a tariff on sugar by which we benefit. Beyond that, there is only the couple of million dollars which the States dump here every month for naval and military expenses."

Sure enough, I soon found pineapples were cheap —on the plantations. One day I bought from a lorry in a street six of them for five cents. But all the same, the greengrocers would have soaked me five cents each for these same pineapples: or ten cents, for very large ones. Evidently John Hop—most of the greengrocers are Chinese—knows a thing or two about the doctrine of profit.

In every country I had yet visited, high tariffs, I had found, had lowered the standard of living. But I will be fair. Here at last was a country that was benefiting by a tariff. If it had not been for the American tariff on sugar, the island would have been altogether broke. It was quite plain that they gained more by the privileges of that tariff than they were losing by having to pay American prices for the things they imported. Hence the general prosperity : hence the number of fine houses in the suburbs : the multitude of motor-cars, and the number of wealthy Oriental traders.

All the same it stands to reason that this prosperity is bought at someone's expense. You cannot pay Peter without robbing Paul : and without doubt there are many families in the United States which can ill afford to pay those few extra dollars per month which the sugar tariff imposes on them.

*   *   *

Among the many kind friends I met in this city was a Mr. Powlinson, the Superintendent of Parks and Recreation Grounds. With him and a few other friends I enjoyed many outings to places of interest. I went with them, for instance, to the Pali Pass, where the Trade Wind—hemmed in by the mountains on both sides—blows with a force sufficient to lift the roof off a house. What a gorgeous, colourful vista of sea, sky, mountain and valley opens out from the top of that pass northward ! Another day I climbed the Coco crater. Like all the craters of this island, it has been extinct

for thousands of years. In form it is a huge trun-
cated cone, open like a horse-shoe on the windward
side. Its bottom has been all silted up, and is over-
grown with shrub : on the eastward side, a curious
stone bridge has been produced by the weathering
of the lava.

Another Sunday I visited the Sacred Falls—a deep
gorge worn in the rock. At times there is hardly a
trickle of water, but it is liable to swell suddenly
when there is rainfall in the hills : and then,
woe betide the traveller caught in the gorge ! For
it is impossible to climb its vertical sides. Therefore the natives had a custom of propitiating the
god of the Falls by crossing two leaves on a rock
(weighing them down with a little stone) when
they had to pass through the gorge. Even Europeans carry out this little rite, and you can see the
crossed leaves everywhere.

*   *   *

Just before I came to Honolulu there was a
project set on foot to rig out a large war canoe in the
native style, and to paddle or sail it across to the
States. This was regarded as so dare-devil a project that a steamer was to be chartered to accompany
the canoe : to report its progress by wireless, and
to stand by in case of emergency. But now my
little boat, far smaller than the projected war canoe,

174

and manned by only a single sailor, came into harbour—bound moreover for the same destination. It killed the canoe scheme outright.

Young folk particularly were interested in my venture ; and I received numerous requests from school-teachers to tell their charges about my voyage. In consequence I gave lectures to about a dozen schools and colleges. But my hearers did not always learn quite the lessons they were intended to. Fired by a spirit of emulation, some local youths stole a yawl anchored near me, and started off haphazard on a cruise to the South Sea Islands !

They had no charts, no food, no drinking-water, and only one week's provisions. But they had provided themselves with a lady, and with three packets of cigarettes. Oddly enough it seems to have been the fear of the cigarettes running short, rather than the food or water, which decided them before very long to turn back !

Then they ran the stolen yawl ashore as carelessly as they had set out—and had plenty of leisure in which to repent of their adventure in gaol.

Among the many people who used to invite me to lunch was a certain University professor. In the course of conversation he asked my religious opinions.

Naturally the answer I gave him was very different from the one I should have given before my voyage started. " I believe in a parental God," I said, " and in the efficacy of prayer."

The professor answered gravely : " It is Man who made God : and he made Him in his own image."

Well : there was a time in my life, very early, when such a statement would have staggered me and shocked me. Again, there had been a time after that when I should have looked upon it as a revelation of the profoundest truth. But now I seemed to have grown beyond both these stages.

" I will grant you," I said, " that it is Man who has made *religions* : every countless creed and faith and doctrine. But what has impelled him to do so ? It is the existence of God which has necessitated it : which has made it inevitable that man at every time and in every clime should *make* (yes, I grant you that word) an image of the God Whom he knows to exist. The very multiplicity of creeds which has resulted is proof of God's existence. So much for rational proof : but I myself have need of none : for personal experience has convinced me that prayer is heard and answered."

" That must have been merely coincidence," he retorted ; " in fact, it would be stranger if such things did *not* happen, now and then."

Well, I had my own view as to whether or not it

could have been coincidence : I have stated the facts in this book about my prayers and their answers fairly, and I leave it to the reader to judge also.

The trouble about the position of the sceptic seems to me that he is caught in a vicious circle. Because he does not believe in God he cannot pray : because he cannot pray he cannot experience answer to prayer : and because he has not experienced answer to prayer, he cannot believe in God.

Yes : most of my life I had been of that same opinion : but now the curtain of darkness seemed to have been rent in my soul, and the shadows of scepticism were melting away. This was bringing peace and rest to my once-tortured soul.

Peace and rest ! That is more than the teachers of atheism can claim to have found ! Notwithstanding their brave front (I admit they can show courage), right in the centre of their minds you cannot but discern a vacancy—something hopeless —something morbid, and despondent. Their very talk about the Mastery of Man lacks sincerity : for you can see—and they know you can see—that they are shutting their eyes, that they are refusing to look at that Mastery in a scientific way ; refusing to ask themselves boldly why that mastery should have value, if nothing else has.

Have dreams and visions, I sometimes wondered, played an even larger part in pre-scientific navigation than they played in my own voyage ? There is no doubt that in early times the Polynesians navigated for immense distances : for the anthropologist will prove to you conclusively that descendants of their race are to be found on all the habitable islands of the Pacific. How did they find their way about ?

There is, in the Bishop Museum at Honolulu, a vast collection of everything appertaining to the Pacific Ocean. Amongst the exhibits is the " Holy Calabash " ; and some think that native navigators used this as a kind of sextant. But more probably it is nothing more than a witch-doctor's device for raising the wind—a kind of Bag of Aeolus. After all, a sextant, even if they had had one (and this is not one), is practically useless without altitude tables and calendars—and I doubt very much if the Polynesians were ever able to construct these !

In part, of course, no doubt they learned to navigate (as I did, towards the end of my voyage) by the flights of ocean-birds ; by the appearance of the water, the prevailing winds of known regions, and such other small but none the less scientific helps. That, however, could not account (as any reader of this voyage will admit) for *all* their achievements. By the flight of birds alone *I* could certainly never have found my way from Sydney to Honolulu !

We are left therefore with only two possible theories. Perhaps the Polynesian was possessed by an instinct akin to that which directs the migration of birds. Or perhaps in some kind of clairvoyant state, visions of distant islands and a clear apprehension of their direction and distance—dreams perhaps far more vivid than any of mine had been in the same kind—were his chief source of knowledge.

And indeed, who can draw a hard-and-fast line between such dreams, and migratory instincts ? Birds and animals, being on a lower plane of consciousness, probably have no such visions : their wings guide them in a certain direction without conscious intention : but what could be more natural than that such a power—if it existed in man—should take a conscious form ? That he should *see* his destination ; and then, through his human will, translate that sight into the necessary actions for getting there ?

*   *   *

I spent five happy weeks in Honolulu, and then, in spite of the onset of winter, decided to be off. At noon on 3rd November, about sixty people

gathered to see me leave. A little miss put a
rose-bud in my buttonhole, and gave me a kiss.

My heart went out to these people. Some had
taken the time off from their office hours : others
had brought me little tokens of friendship, good-
will, and remembrance. The world cannot be a
bad place to live in when such people are about.

One friend had tried to dissuade me from carrying on, in face of the winter storms, in so frail a
craft. He offered to buy my boat and pay my fare
to America. I had done enough, he said, in getting
as far as I had. But I said no : I was going on with
my task for two reasons : first, because I had undertaken it, and second because it seemed to me an
admirable training for other tasks in life.

Ahead of me now lay the longest lap of my whole
voyage : the passage from the Sandwich Islands to
the American coast. This was two thousand two
hundred miles, as the crow flies : but it would
mean at least three thousand miles of sailing
distance : a distance equal to the distance from
New York to Liverpool.

I was towed down the harbour and away.

In Honolulu I had overhauled my food stores.
Much of the food I had brought with me from
Australia was still in good condition (even some
slightly weevilly rice which I had bought in Suva
180

had got no worse : the weevils I suppose were stifled in my air-tight containers). Moreover, following the famous Harry Pidgeon's example, I carried with me two bushels of wheat ; and this too was still sound.

The possible uses of this wheat were many. Sometimes I would grind a little of it fresh to mix with my flour, when making bread. In an emergency, of course, I could have lived on boiled wheat as Australian farmers do. And there were other uses for it. If I had felt the lack of vitamins, I could have sprouted the wheat for greens.

For the question of vitamins, if you would avoid scurvy, is one of the most important points in victualling for a long voyage. One thing I used to do on this account was to add a little bean-meal to the dough when I was making bread : then, before baking it, I would ferment it till it went slightly acid.

One's taste is a very fair judge of the healthiness of one's diet ; and this acid bread, when fried in olive oil, satisfied my taste for weeks together. If it had not been healthy I should have tired of it without doubt : but I did not.

CHAPTER XV

My Watches Prove Unreliable—Reading and Meditation—
A December Cyclone—The Sea-anchor Fails—Cross-seas—
On her Beam-ends—" I am in Trouble, Birdie ! "—The
Centre-board as Drogue—Wells or the Bible—Prayer—
The Gale Moderates—Lovely Sailing Weather—My Thoughts
Fly to Lady-fancies—I Lose all Knowledge of my Longi-
tude—Christmas at Sea—Another Gale—Disbelief is Elastic
—New Year's Day, 1933—Prayer Answered Again—Why
it did not Convince Me—A Vision—January 3rd : the Coast
of America Sighted—The Lamp—Becalmed—January 8th,
1933, My Voyage Ends

ON the morning of 11th November I was romping
along under full sail when the U.S. army transport
St. Michael came up astern, and passed a few
chains to leeward of me. The crew and the men
on board lined the rail, cheered and waved. The
Captain hailed me, asked how I was, and gave
me my latitude and longitude. These, however,
were of little use to me so early in my passage :
it is towards the end of a passage that you really
want to know where you are. Moreover, with so
wide an objective as the American coast, I was not
sailing any particular compass course—just edging
along, to the north and east, as the wind suited.

My Watches Prove Unreliable

As I advanced northward, however, it began to be uncomfortably cold. To avoid a chill I cut up a woollen blanket, and made it into two shirts. The winds were blowing harder, and the sea was getting rougher. Often when taking in a reef I would get a ducking : and then the wet clothes had to dry on my back. At one time I felt very near to pneumonia ; but I took what precautions I could, and it passed off. Chilblains, however, appeared on my toes—which were always bare, and generally wet.

Both my watches were going now : but sometimes one of them would lose or gain, sometimes the other. If my taffrail-log had been functioning I could have probably spotted the culprit : but without this means of checking them I was at a loss, and could not tell with exactitude what progress I was making in my easting. I could not get the time by lunar observations such as I had used on the Equator (after missing Jarvis), because of the rough seas, and because in this more northerly latitude the meridian altitudes were too low.

Well, I just had to take things as they came : and to be content with the hope that I should reach some part of the American shore some day.

I was well supplied with reading matter on this leg of my voyage. As usual, it was the heavy stuff requiring thought which agreed with me best.

I finished reading the Bible through : and then I read from cover to cover H. G. Wells's bulky *Outline of History*. I must confess that the latter book left a nasty taste in my mouth. For what is this " outline," but an interminable catalogue of violence and cruelty ? A welter of blood, and the eternal struggle of Man for supremacy. In comparison even the hungry shark in the ocean seemed to me less brutal than some of these human heroes, who have butchered their fellow-kind—nailed them to the cross—tortured them on the rack—burned them at the stake.

If I were to judge by Wells's record, the thin veneer of modern civilization has not changed the original brutal nature of man. All life is an incessant struggle for dominion and power, and the moment strength fails comes overthrow.

It is a gloomy and hopeless outlook. If fifty thousand years of human existence have not succeeded in improving man's nature above that of a shark or tiger, what chance is there of any betterment taking place in the near future ?

But I knew very well, from my own experience, that this estimate of human character is not the true one. Indeed, if I had really believed the world to be inhabited by nothing but predatory brutes I should have had no wish to go on living in it : I should just have stepped over the side of my boat. But throughout my voyage it had been proved to me, again and again, that there is good in the world, and fine people living in it. Utter stranger though I was, they went out of their way to do me kindness. Such people I believe have always existed in the world, perhaps formed a large proportion of its population. It is just that they never make enough noise and fuss to get into history-books like Mr. Wells's—that is all.

Again, according to Wells, Christ was Man, not God. Wells is graciously ready to hand him a bouquet for enriching the realm of philosophy with the " Kingdom of God " idea—but that is all. For the rest, Wells does not seem to think Christianity so good a religion as several other of the Asiatic creeds.

If this was all Christ did, it was not much : for even the Kingdom of God idea was not wholly original : the Pharisees had some such notion already.

Years ago, when my own views coincided with those expressed by Mr. Wells, I should have swallowed everything he said without further thought. But now I had plenty of time to con it over.

* * *

On 10th December I ran into a cyclone. The wind veered round from north-east to south-east, and then blew with gale force. The next day it suddenly stopped for a couple of hours (meaning that I was in the centre), then it began again from the south and once more veered round to north-east, from which point the gusts were presently terrific.

From hour to hour the gale grew stronger. I tried my sea-anchor, but it could not keep my boat head on to the breakers. This was because the centre-board was set rather far aft : it acted as a pivot, and so the boat had a tendency to pay off before the breakers, a tendency which was too strong for the drogue to overcome.

Next I tried the treble-reefed mainsail, sheeted hard amidships. This proved more effective in keeping the boat's nose into the waves. In that position she could stand almost any seas. Sometimes the breakers would fly right over the boat's whole length in a solid sheet of water ; but they never swamped her.

Unfortunately, however, waves are not always regular : sometimes a nasty cross-sea would catch her broadside, and come in over the gunwale. Then I would have to get busy with the bailer. How high these seas really were I cannot tell : for it is hard to judge in a little boat. But they seemed mountainous, and very steep.

On the morning of 13th December a particularly nasty breaker struck the boat broadside. For a moment I thought she was going to turn right over ; for she stood on her beam ends, with the sea pouring in over both gunwales at once. Thanks to the heavy centre-board, however, she righted herself. Instantly I was out from my waterlogged bunk to take a look round. I expected to see that angry breaker continue its onward rush. But the sea to leeward was comparatively smooth : only a few acres of broken milky water all around me. When that brute hit the boat it had spent its own force, instead of destroying me ! Some damage it had done, however—the rudder pintles were bent, and the tiller broken off short.

The boat was half full of water, too ; so I bailed her out before setting to work to repair the tiller. While I was doing this a sea-gull came and settled on the waves a few yards astern. He was watching me, so I said to him, " I am in trouble, birdie ; I would feel much safer right now if I was in your skin ! "

To make matters worse I found that the sea-anchor (it had been given to me in Honolulu) was gone. I had belayed it to the fore-deck, but the seas which had been breaking over the bows all night had broken the lashings and carried it away.

Something had to be done : the gale still kept rising ; louder and more insistent grew its shrieks in the rigging.

The only thing I could think of to make a sea-anchor with was the centre-board. So I hauled it up : fastened it to the bows by two long ropes : and dumped it overboard. It did not act as well as it should have done, for it kept slewing from side to side : but all the same it kept the boat facing up to the breakers much better than the sail was then doing alone.

It was not till then that I realized what serious danger I was in. With the centre-board taken out there was nothing any longer to right the boat, and she showed a tendency to capsize : in fact, should another cross-sea hit her now, the centre-board would even add to the trouble.

There was still another hour till sunset, and the promise of a bad night. The barometer was lower than ever, and still falling : every gust of the gale sounded a more threatening note.

What if my boat did capsize, and dawn found me a derelict ? I should be without hope of rescue, for I had not seen a ship for weeks.

It was at this moment that Wells's denial of the Divinity of Christ came back to my mind. What a splendid opportunity this was to settle the question !

According to Wells Christ was but a mere man. Now Wells is unquestionably a person of great ability, intellect, and education. He is an authority on history and a famous novelist to boot ; and he is greatly esteemed in all American educational circles. I could not, therefore, but regard his opinion as carrying weight—not lightly to be disregarded. On the other hand the Bible claims Divinity for Christ : according to the Bible, by His mere command He healed the sick, raised the dead, calmed the storm on the Sea of Galilee, and did many other wonderful things. Also He had said : "Whatsoever you ask of the Father in My Name He will give it you." And the Bible also has been highly esteemed by many able, intellectual, educated men, at one time or another. So the question now in my mind was, which was the liar, Wells or the Bible ? One of them must be.

I might have read a thousand books and yet their reading could never have answered that question. Only a practical test could answer it—such a test as the present storm afforded.

I knew my boat : she was a good boat, but I knew that she was no match for this gale. I knew I was in danger of my life, and my need a pressing one. But had I not left Australia in a little boat with the very object in view, that I might test Providence ? That I might find out for sure if there is a God Who cares for us ? I felt rather agitated : for the next hour, I felt, would be—in both senses—the most decisive in my life. Then I said the following prayer :

" God Almighty, I know Thou hearest me. I am in need, and I am in doubt. I am in danger of death : and I want to know if Christ really was what He claimed to be. Therefore, as a test I ask Thee *in the Name of Jesus Christ*, please moderate this gale before sunset."

I know that most people will laugh at the idea of anyone trying to stop a tempest by prayer. Yet the words were hardly out of my mouth when the gale began to ease off. The sting seemed gone out of the angry blasts, and ever rarer did they come. By sunset it was no more than a moderate breeze which kept on easing off all the night. By eight o'clock next morning there was not a breath of breeze left. It was the abruptest knock-out to any gale I had ever witnessed.

Notwithstanding my wet bed and clothing I slept peaceably that night : and was only twice awakened by heavy splashes coming in over the side—both of which gave my head and pillow another sousing.

In the morning the sea presented the strangest appearance I had ever seen. The air was dead calm, but a mountainous glassy swell still ran, denoting that the centre of the disturbance had shifted in a north-westerly direction. The waves showed no signs of breaking : and through the unruffled sides of these giant billows one could see deep into their sombre depths.

The barometer had commenced to rise : the storm was plainly over. I set to work to rig the centre-board once more. It was a harder job than I had anticipated ; for it is one thing to lift a heavy weight by a direct hold, but a very different thing to handle the same weight on a wet rope. It was not till I rigged a purchase with a couple of little pulley-blocks that I managed yard by yard to yank the centre-board up on to the foredeck. Even then I had more trouble, working it aft and getting it into position. Once that was done I felt much relieved.

Meanwhile the sun had come out clear and warm, so I took the opportunity of hoisting all my wet bedding and clothes on to a line ; and by the afternoon I had them fairly dry.

That evening a moderate following breeze set in, and continued for over a week.

I found this last lap of my voyage more lonely than any sailing that I had yet done. I had plenty of magazines to read, plenty of books to study : and I spent much time writing. But still I longed badly for human company—for the first time. My memory would fly back to all the lady-fancies that had ever come into my life ; but I found them all faded, except one—that one whose features seemed to be for ever engraved upon my mind—

Elaine! Our paths had crossed, never to meet again ; and yet I could not forget her.

*   *   *

On the night of 17th December I heard a throbbing noise ; and on looking out I saw, about two miles away, the lights of a motor-ship on a southerly course. In the forenoon of the next day a big mailboat passed, in the same direction. She seemed to turn a little off her course towards my boat : but as I gave no signals she continued on her way. Plainly I was crossing the San Francisco-Panama steamer-track.

The day after that a school of what at first I took to be sharks came up astern. But as they passed ahead I recognized them to be dolphins. For a while they amused themselves by cutting circles round my boat and by shooting past its bow. But soon they disappeared.

Another morning I was startled by hearing a heavy blowing, like the letting off of steam from a boiler. It was a whale, about half a mile astern— the only one I ever sighted.

Birds were now becoming more plentiful and varied : some were types that I had never seen before.

On the 22nd December, according to my longitude calculations I was somewhere in the middle of the town of San Diego. But there was no land in sight. Evidently my watches had gained more than I had allowed for : so there was nothing for it but to continue sailing to the east, knowing that sooner or later I must reach land.

Actually it was twelve days before I sighted any. If it had been some low coral shore that I was running towards, a shore which perhaps could only be seen for a few miles off, imagine the strain of those twelve days and nights ! But fortunately the Californian coast is a high one—visible for at least thirty miles : so that if I had not sighted land at sun-down I could turn in with reasonable certainty that I should not run aground in the night.

December is a bad month on the Californian coast, and I had by no means finished with gales. On Christmas Eve some nasty squalls set in, and all the next day the weather grew worse. Again I had to heave-to, under treble-reefed mainsail : and all this time the northerly blow was driving me to the southward of my course. That was the most miserable Christmas I have ever spent.

By the morning of the 28th December things looked very bad indeed. To the north, a number of compressed dark clouds resembling vultures or aeroplanes in formation were bearing down on me, and the gale was howling a treat. Once more a nasty cross-sea hit my boat and the tiller broke in my hand. I had to repair it, then and there, as best I could. Meanwhile, the merciless blasts were giving such a drubbing to the treble-reefed mainsail that soon it was in ribbons.

So this sail, which had served me faithfully for over a year, was at last done for !

At the very height of the gale I had to strip its ragged remains off the spars and bend the spare. This was a second-hand sail which had been given me in Suva ; it looked mildewed, and I felt great anxiety lest it too should tear to ribbons and leave me with no sail at all. Yet without it I could not do the one necessary thing—keep *Elaine* with her bows into the seas. I had a sea-anchor out—just a kite like the first one, made by lashing a spare jib to two crossed oars. But it soon smashed up. Then I lowered the boat's anchor from the bows in a bag. That too helped to keep her facing the breakers, until the bag was torn from the anchor's flukes.

Taking it all in all, I was sorely pressed by that gale, and felt that things were liable to get nasty at any time. It was a pity, I thought, to have my boat wrecked and my journey stopped so near my goal. Besides, life may still be worth living. " Not a hair falls of your head without the Father's knowledge," had said Christ : if my life was in danger then surely God must be aware of it.

It had certainly seemed that the last gale had

moderated in answer to my prayer. *Seemed*, I say ; for I was not, even yet, convinced. Disbelief is elastic as india-rubber : once the pressure of evidence is released, back it springs to its former position. Doubts were still nibbling at my soul. Suppose it had just been a coincidence ? Suppose I just happened to pray when the gale was about to abate of its own accord ?

Well, I had a fine chance now for a second test. So I prayed again exactly as before.

Once more the result was the same. By sunset the gale had sufficiently moderated to allow me to sail all through the night under storm canvas : and for the next three days there was as fine sailing weather as you could wish.

But on New Year's Eve the wind freshened again ; and on 1st January, 1933, it was once more blowing a gale. That gale blew out my storm jib : and while I was mending the canvas I decided to give prayer one more test.

This case was different from the other two. There was no pressing need : this was just a mere gale of wind : I was not in mortal danger. In fact it looked as if I was becoming a regular cadger with the Almighty—and deserved to be treated as a cadger. But had not Christ said, " *Whatsoever* you ask of the Father . . . you shall have it " ? I just wanted to test that statement.

195

H

Besides, why *should* I be battling with gales, when for all the harm it could do anybody else I might as well have fair sailing weather ?

So once more I prayed in Christ's name for a moderating of the gale, and for fair sailing weather. Let me have it by noon, I asked : and then I settled down contentedly expecting it to happen.

That afternoon the gale went down : a following breeze set in, and continued till I came within sight of land. However, with the wind dead aft my boat was hard to keep on her course. She yawed about and showed a tendency to gybe : so, to keep her head steady, I rigged an extension to the bowsprit ; and set a spare jib spinnaker-fashion.

You might have thought that after so many of my prayers had been answered there could no longer be any room for doubts in my head : and if I confess the opposite you will lose patience with me. But so it was. Doubt is hard to kill. While I prayed, my faith would soar high—till it seemed that an answer *could not* be withheld. But no sooner was it all over and I had got what I asked, than my faith would slump right down to the zero-mark. Partly this was because the answers seemed in each case to come so naturally : nothing of the miraculous about them, as we understand the miraculous—no clatter or banging.

There seemed no end to the amount of corrob-

196

oration my faith needed : to the piling up of miracle on miracle. I suppose that was what the old Jews felt, who in spite of all the miracles Christ had already performed, yet came to Him and asked Him for a sign.

But before long the reason for my dissatisfaction with these repeated proofs dawned upon my mind. Each time, what I had prayed for was an earthly thing. The answer, therefore, could be no proof of a heavenly thing. Somehow the text came into my mind : " When I go to the Father I will send you a Witness—the Holy Ghost, Who shall testify of Me." That, I felt, was the imperative need. If that Holy Spirit was in the world to-day then I must find It, and make room for It within me. Without that Spirit no mere answer to prayer for material needs could satisfy me.

For what did it benefit my *soul* to receive such things by prayer, any more than by skill or science ?

It was something else I needed : so my prayer went up : " O God in Heaven, lead me, guide and enlighten me, that I blunder not in my quest of Thee."

* * *

That night as my boat was borne quietly along by the gentle breeze I had a strange and vivid dream—the last of my dreams that I shall record here.

I seemed to be above the deck : and with a clearness quite unusual in a dream I saw the moonlight playing upon the hood of my boat. It was so clear, I could see the texture of the canvas of which the hood was made. But there was something mysterious about the scene ; for though I could see the bellied sail I could feel no breeze. Though I could see the rippling ocean all round me I could not *hear* the wavelets lapping, as the little white-caps noiselessly disappeared under the hull of the boat. Yet this gave me no alarm. I only remember how deserted the boat looked ; an outside observer would never suspect someone was asleep there, under the hood.

Then I found myself rising obliquely : and from an elevation of about one hundred feet I caught sight of the boat once more. She looked smaller now, and I beheld a wider expanse of the moonlit sea—with dark blotches on it here and there where the moonlight was obscured by a cloud. Higher and higher I seemed to rise, through clouds and mists, till at last the horizon disappeared. Then at last there was nothing above me but the moon shining out of a clear sky : and beneath me an ocean, not of water, but of clouds.

Yet I rose still higher, till dawn seemed to break in the *west*, and the sun rose above the horizon beneath which he had so lately sunk. I must have risen high indeed, for that appearance ! But higher still : and then the westerly rim of the world shone like the sickle of some giant moon—a moon which even then was growing visibly smaller. It was not many more moments before moon, earth and sun all dwindled and disappeared out of sight. Now there was nothing all round me but the midnight sky lit by a multitude of brilliant stars.

Yet my motion did not cease, as I soared past constellations. I saw new planets and new suns. What force was it, I wondered, that in a kind of mighty pulsation thus bore me upward ? For I felt as if I were carried in the hands of some very powerful friendly being : but I could not see him, neither could I very well see my body—or whatever visible shape my soul might then be wearing. For it seemed to be garbed in a sort of night-shift from which came a faint light ; and from which there spread downwards, in the direction I had come from, a thin slightly wavy and speckled luminous ribbon—a ribbon clipped, as it were, from the Milky Way.

Tremendous as the distance seemed, I must have traversed it with the speed of thought, for it did not take me half the time to travel it that I have taken to relate it now.

But presently a new sun, brighter than the one we see from Earth, came into view. Rather, it was only half a sun : for the right half seemed to be obscured by some sort of screen.

Rays emanated from it and shone upon surrounding clouds ; but at the same time I realized that this was no ordinary star of the sky. For those rays conveyed not heat nor light, but love ! It was when one of those rays fell upon me that I discerned this : immediately the sense of love was kindled in my heart. Then, as they shone more fully upon me this love grew into a deep, fervent passion : resembling, and yet surpassing, the joy and exhilaration a man feels when he meets once again the person he loves best, after a separation of a long time.

It was strange to me, this, to find that my heart was capable of burning with love for something that wore the look of an inanimate object—a sun. Yet for me it was the joy of Heaven to bask in the rays of this sun of love. Moments of time were spun out into oblivion, so that I cannot say how long I tarried in that state of happiness : all I know is that I wanted to remain there for ever.

But consciousness was stealing upon me that I could not do so as yet. Some bond still seemed to hold me to an earthly existence : I felt that I still had something to do in the world. At that, presently I found myself sinking, sinking, and again sinking.

To my ears again came the soft lapping of wavelets under the hull of the boat ; and I woke to find myself in my bunk aboard the *Elaine*.

That truly had been a wonderful dream, I thought.

*   *   *

There were now indications that my boat was getting close to land. A few sea-gulls were following me : and if I threw them a piece of bread they would swoop down and swallow it (in mid-ocean it is seldom that a sea-gull will touch bread).

Then a match, too : one of those big, fat, American matches. I saw it floating past the boat one morning, so I knew that land must be near. Luckily there was no fog about, though it is apt to obscure the Californian coast at this time of year.

It was early on 3rd January, 1933, that I sighted land. My landfall turned out to be San Nicholas Island, about eighty miles south-west from San Pedro, the harbour of Los Angeles.

A week ago I should have been overjoyed to see it : but now that I had been so long wearied with vain expectation I felt no exhilaration whatever. I went on with my tasks all day long as if the land did not exist.

By a sight of the sun I now found that my watches had gained an hour and twenty-seven minutes on the run, thereby putting my bearings out by nearly one thousand miles ! If ever I go off for another cruise I shall most certainly see to it that I have a more reliable time-keeper on board—or else a radio receiver, to catch the time-signals.

I was now right in the track of the many steamers which go in and out of Los Angeles Harbour : so it was only prudent that I should carry a light by night. I spent a couple of hours trying to solder a new bottom to my old lantern—for the old bottom had rusted through. But I could not make much of a job at it.

Next morning, I was becalmed for a couple of hours twelve miles east of San Nicholas Island. Presently my attention was caught by a pole bobbing up and down in the water a few chains away. Becoming curious I rowed over to it, and pulled it out of the water. It was a long bamboo pole with a white flag tied to one end, and a hurricane lantern tied to its middle. Well, I certainly never expected to get a lantern out of the ocean ! Not once in a thousand years would anyone fish a lantern out of the ocean—and particularly so if he happened to be in need of one. Surely our Father in Heaven knows our needs. He does not only answer our prayers (I had not prayed for any lantern), but supplies them before we ask !

Becalmed

Now the wind totally died away, and for the next three days my boat lay becalmed between Catalina Island and San Pedro ; and those three nights the lantern sent by Providence burned brightly at the mast-head.

It was tantalizing to see the harbour in the distance : to watch steamers going in and out, and yet to be unable to sail in. A pall of smoke hung about, and was wafted back and forth out of Long Beach Bay. Sometimes a steamer would come out of San Pedro Harbour, and—as if the air were not thick enough already—would leave a long streak of black smoke in its wake which would slowly diffuse in the stagnant air.

The sun rose in a brown east, and set in a brown west.

Having breathed pure air for the last two months the smoke almost choked me.

By the midnight following 7th January my boat was within half a mile of the harbour entrance, when once more the little breeze failed ; and so I turned in to snatch an hour's rest. I was wakened as if by the rushing of a gale : and on looking out saw barely a chain away the stern of a steamer that had shot past me. It made me glad that I had a light burning on my boat's mast : for without it I might easily be run down.

A very little while after, a slight draught set in,

and within two hours I was inside the harbour. Spotting a mooring near Cabrillo Beach I made fast to it.

My boat voyage was complete. The frail *Elaine* had brought me more than eight thousand miles across the Pacific. As I turned in to sleep again that night, I felt like pinching myself to make sure that it was not a dream : that I had in real truth reached my destination.

A year and a week had passed since I left Sydney. Out of this time I had spent some five months on shore on the islands, each day of which had been a pleasure to me. Of the seven months that I had actually spent at sea, maybe I was totally becalmed for a dozen days : maybe I weathered about a dozen gales. I still had four months' supply of food left when I reached Los Angeles : two months' supply of water. Boat and gear had cost me all told one hundred and twenty-five dollars ; food, spares, and replacements had cost me one hundred dollars for the year. Should I ever go on another such voyage I would choose a decked-in boat, bigger and more comfortable than the *Elaine*. And yet she had served me faithfully : and I was sorry for the fate that befell her three days later.

PART III

★

THE AFTERMATH

CHAPTER XVI

*Los Angeles—Red Tape—" The Regulations are Lousy ! "—
Publicity—I Refuse to Lecture—Elaine Wrecked in Harbour
—The Immigration Department—Cunning Questions—Harry
Pidgeon—I am Arrested—Graft in the Immigration
Department—How the Wretched Immigrant is Bled—
Behind Bars—Released on Recognizances*

ON the morning of the 8th January, having waited
in vain a couple of hours for the Quarantine Officer
to arrive, I asked a passing boatman to ring up
the Harbour Master's office.

Word came back for me to stay where I was : that
the Quarantine launch would be along presently.
Actually it did not come till three o'clock in the
afternoon. I was asked enough questions to fill a
newspaper column—and then billed five dollars for
the privilege of answering them.

I protested that I had paid my Quarantine fees
already in Honolulu : why should I be charged
again at another United States port ?

They answered that I would have been exempt
had I come from another American port on the
mainland : but coming from Honolulu I had to
pay again. Those were the regulations.

" Considering that Americans on single-handed voyages have been exempted from harbour dues in foreign ports without exception over the whole world, *I* think the regulations are lousy."

The doctor seemed embarrassed.

My arrival appeared to create quite a stir. A fortnight before, several newspapers had reported that I had perished in the December gales. Now that I had turned up alive I was naturally besieged by reporters and private questioners also, and received many invitations ashore. They came and took pictures of me for the news-reels also.

One man who spoke to me was very frank. " I have come down from Hollywood specially to see you," he said : " and I do not mind saying I am a bit disappointed. I thought you would have looked a bit more of a buccaneer : but you are such a mild-looking chap, you don't look different from anybody else."

I could not help laughing. " That's it," I said : " fierceness doesn't pay on a voyage like that. Your buccaneer would probably have gone to the bottom long ago."

Offers of various kinds came rolling in. A Lecture Agent wanted to engage me, boat and all, for a lecture tour of the United States. But I did not like the idea : it would involve too much skiting and bragging, so I turned it down. It would have meant a lot of money probably : it might have set me up for life : but I did not want setting up for life. Once you are set up for life, living is more or less over. If I had accepted that offer this book might have ended right here. There would have been nothing more of any interest to anybody in the life of Fred Rebell. As it is you will see there are quite a few pages left. Moreover, I had not got yet where I wanted to. My boat was in a United States port, that is true : but I knew very well that my soul was not in port yet. The spirit within me had still many perils, many gales and head-winds to face before it should drop its anchor for the last time in anything that could be really called shelter. And I have yet to hear of the man who could think about his soul and God Almighty while on an American lecture platform.

My boat was in harbour : but yet she was not safe. That may come as a bit of a surprise to landsmen who think once a boat is in port all you have to do is to tie her up to the steps and go ashore and forget about her. The sailor knows, however, that a boat needs just as much watching and care in harbour as she does at sea : the safety is relative only : and there are certain dangers in harbour which do not arise in the open : in fact circumstances may be such that to seek safety you may actually have to put out of harbour into the open once more.

On the night of 10th January there was a heavy fog over the harbour, and fog-sirens were blowing on the San Pedro breakwater. I was sleeping on board, of course. About midnight I was woken up by a strong blow that had set in from the south-east. Now the harbour is unprotected from that direction, and I felt uneasy. Only a few weeks before they had had a heavy south-easterly gale —what they call a Santiana—and a number of boats had been wrecked right inside the harbour itself.

Within an hour there was a sixty-mile-per-hour gale blowing, still from the south-east : the seas were breaking heavily on the shore, and my boat was jerking at her mooring-lines. Should they part I would be blown up on the beach. I got up and put out the anchor—in case.

Moreover, I put two reefs in the mainsail : for if the mooring-lines parted there was little hope that a single anchor would hold her : and then the only thing to do would be to try to beat out to the open sea. It would be a choice between that and running ashore—and in those pounding breakers *Elaine* would not stand much chance, once she touched the ground. But if only I could make

210

the open sea—I had after all ridden out gales like
this before.

However, I never had a chance. The mooring-
lines parted and the anchor dragged : and I could
not make out to sea because I was too close on to
the shore already—right in the breakers. The
wind was blowing dead on to the shore : it would
have been a dead beat to get out : those breakers
were tossing her about like a chip : there was no
chance of getting steerage way on her.

So I just stood helpless waiting for the end.
" God have mercy on me," I muttered : and in spite
of the sour look things wore I had a kind of inner
conviction that this would not be the end for me.

A few moments later my boat was alongside
two big piles. If a wave had lifted her then and
dashed her against them she would have been
smashed to bits : but no, she seemed to halt and
then slip gently in between them.

The next danger was a jetty which I narrowly
missed—that too would have smashed her to match-
wood, and me with her, had she hit. But somehow she drifted round into comparative shelter.
Then for the first time I felt her touch bottom.
Every breaker that came picked her up bodily, and
carried her farther up the shore : till presently she
stuck fast and between waves I was able to jump
out on to *terra firma*.

211

Even ashore like this she still rode upright. All this while her heavy centre-board of half-inch iron had been down : I never got a chance to haul it up. Bumping, the plate bent at right angles without splitting the keel : and now made a kind of shoe on which she sat as straight as if legged up on a slipway !

However, the gale and the tide both were still rising, so I set about getting on shore what of my belongings I could.

While I was doing this a naval launch, fully manned and with her motor running, came drifting past. She too had broken her moorings. Well, if a naval motor-launch could not make out to sea in the teeth of this gale it was not surprising that I had been unable to make any headway beating against it under double-reefed mainsail.

It was this naval launch which did the damage. First she broke my bowsprit : then she bumped into *Elaine* time after time, straining her bow, breaking a number of her ribs, and starting several leaks. When the damage was done she too ran ashore and her crew landed.

We were not the only sufferers, of course. About thirty boats in all — yachts and launches — broke their moorings that night and were blown ashore : and two lives were lost. For those Santianas are not common : the following winter there were

212

none : and this particular one, coming so close on the heels of the previous one, took everybody unprepared. The beach was soon covered with other sailormen besides myself, soused and sorry. Presently we all dossed down for the night in the boat-house office.

During the night the gale eased off : but the rising sun lit a sordid sight. The beach was strewn with piles of debris, and over a score of small wrecks. My own boat was high and dry : and thanks to the attentions of the naval launch unfit to take the water again : so for the time being I put up at the boat-house. I was there, sitting on what I had been able to save of my belongings, when I had a message from the Immigration Department : would I please pay them a call ?

I knew well enough that my lack of a properly visaed passport meant that I was bound to strike trouble anyway. Well, you may as well be hung for a sheep as a lamb, so I decided to take a high line with them. Moreover, I was genuinely curious to see what would happen. I had already pitted my will against the forces of nature, and won. Now I was about to pit my will against the forces of a great nation—as expressed in its laws. Which would win this time ?

The examiner at the Immigration Department asked me how long I meant to stay in the country.

I attempted no evasion: " Eight months," I said.

He asked me if I was aware that the law forbade my doing so without a properly visaed passport. I told him flat that I had as much right on American soil as he had. " Why ? " said he. " Were you born here ? "

" I was born in this round world," I answered : " and this is only a part of it."

" O-ho," said he, " then you do not believe in government ? "

" On the contrary," I answered, " I certainly consider that governments are necessary to safeguard life and property."

" Then you disapprove of the Democratic Government of the United States ? " he asked next.

" Your government is far from perfect," I answered.

All this time, of course, he was trying to catch me out under the clause which forbids anarchists and those who believe in upsetting an established government by force to land in the United States. His next few questions showed this clearer.

" Well, if you want to change our government, how do you propose to bring that change about ? "

I answered seriously that I had not come round to considering that yet.

214

" Are you a Communist ? " he asked me.

" No," said I : " I have no sympathy for Communism."

" Have you ever taken part in any political movement ? "

" Never."

There was nothing he could properly hold against me in all that !

" Have you got a religion ? " he asked.

" Yes," said I, " I am a Christian."

Then he changed his tactics. " You were admitted at Honolulu on a sixty days' permit as a seaman : are you prepared to leave this country as a seaman when your permit expires ? "

" No," said I. " I do not propose signing on under any other master than myself : and the United States Navy has wrecked my boat."

Next I assured him when I did come to leave I was willing to do so at my own expense : I was not looking for a free passage.

" If you were ordered to leave this country within two months, would you obey that order ? " This question was unfair : for if he was prepared to let me stay in the country for two months he ought to have waited that time to see whether or not I would leave at the end of it. But I had no intention of quibbling.

" No," I said : " I need more than two months

for what I have to do." Thus I voluntarily gave
him the advantage he had been seeking all this
time.

" So," he said triumphantly : " if you were
ordered to leave you would not ? Well, in that
case there is nothing for it but to put you under
arrest."

" The law demands it ? " I asked.

" The law demands it," he answered.

" Well," said I, " then as long as you believe
that humanity is made to serve the law, and not
the law made to serve humanity, I agree that you
have no alternative."

So I was put under arrest. In the outer offices
one of the officers seemed surprised. " What are
you arresting him for ? " he asked.

" He made his own passport," said the examiner,
" and he has no respect for constituted government."

Respect ? Respect is not a feeling you can
conjure up at will. If something or somebody
shows itself worthy of respect, then I feel respect :
but if something shows itself just plumb crazy how
am I to feel respect for that ? " By their fruits ye
shall know them." A man might as well be asked
to feel respect for a drunk trying to stand on
his head in a fire-bucket as to feel respect for the
Sovereign Democratic Government of the United

216

States of America, as revealed by that Government's Immigration laws.

*   *   *

I told them that my property was lying about unprotected in the boat-house, and asked permission to go to see to it. As a matter of fact, all the money I possessed was loose in the pocket of my spare trousers there. But I was not allowed to go that night, which I spent in the Detention Barracks. Next morning they let me go to see to it in the company of two detectives: and luckily, though the place had been open all night, my money was still there.

In the meanwhile, Harry Pidgeon, one of the most famous single-handed sailors the world has ever known, who circumnavigated the globe, and whose story had been one of the inspirations of my own venture, had heard of my arrival and came hot-foot to bid me welcome. He arrived to find me already enjoying his country's hospitality under the care of two detectives. "Harry," said I, "in the whole of your voyage, were you ever treated by any government in the world as I am being treated?"

"Never," he said emphatically.

Now one of the detectives chipped in: "*You* had a passport, and proper papers," he said.

" If I had," said Harry Pidgeon hotly, " no one
ever asked to see them ! "

When I got back to the Immigration Barracks
I found that a warrant had already arrived from
Washington for my arrest. The charge was that
I had already overstayed my time in the States.
This was looking ahead a bit. Including the time
I had spent in Honolulu I had not yet been
fifty days in the States out of the sixty allowed to
me by my seaman's permit. This seemed to me
a point which I might do well to consult a lawyer
upon, so my hearing was adjourned for a week.
This week I spent under lock and key in the
Immigration Barracks at San Pedro.

At the beginning of the last chapter I said that
if I had accepted the Lecture Agent's offer this
story would have been at an end : I should have
had nothing more of interest to relate. But these
Immigration Barracks contained far more of interest
than any American lecture hall or Ladies' Club.
One of the things which surprised me was the
number of men detained here who were being
detained by their own free will. They *wanted* to
be deported. There was one Scotsman, for instance,
who had been in the country for thirteen years.
Lately, on account of the depression, he had been
mostly unemployed : and now he figured on a free
passage home to Scotland. But the last thing the

Photo : Stanley Wheeler : " Los Angeles Herald and Express "

Digging the " Elaine " out of sand

*Two single-handed sailors : Harry Pidgeon and the author at San
    Pedro, California, 1933*

law is for, of course, is to do to a man what he wants. Just because this Scotsman wanted to leave the States he could not do so. They set him free : and turned him out into the streets without a penny in his pockets just before the dinner-bell went.

I do not suppose that prisoners anywhere love their warders, and much of what I heard in that place I discounted on those grounds. One man— he was going a little crazy I think—went so far as to maintain that in order to get incriminating evidence out of him they doctored his food, causing him acute bodily discomfort : and served him with soap which made his hair fall out. I am not refer- ring to stories of that kind, which I can disbelieve as easily as you can. But of one thing there seemed abundant evidence : that graft was no stranger to the Immigration Department.

It was a well-educated German who let me into the secret of it. The wretched alien is looked on as a sort of milch cow, to be milked dry by the skilful dairyman. The system of granting bail is how it is done.

" First," he said, " they arrest you on some trumped-up charge. They know your financial standing probably better than you know it yourself : and bail is fixed at a figure which they know you cannot pay. That forces you into the hands of a Bail Company. First you have to fork out ten per cent. of the amount of bail fixed—the officials know very well that you have that much. This ten per cent. you pay to the Bail Company, and it is non-returnable : and the officials, of course, get their whack out of it. As for the rest of the bail, it is never paid at all. All the Bail Company does is to guarantee the other ninety per cent., and their guarantee is accepted instead of cash."

This friend of mine had been particularly unlucky : for after he had paid his ten per cent. the Bail Company had gone bankrupt, and in consequence he was once more under arrest. He had gained nothing, by being granted bail, but a few days' freedom : and was fifty dollars poorer.

I made up my mind that no Bail Company should line its pockets with the contents of mine : I would stay where I was. And indeed, life in the barracks themselves was not too bad. We had two meals a day and we were not without diversion. One evening, for instance, we staged a debate on the well-worn subject, " Has Capitalism Failed ? " The motion was proposed and seconded by two avowed Communists, and opposed by a Hindu student who was to be deported because he had overstayed his permit and had been found working for a living. And perhaps it will comfort the solid citizens of America to know that we—this dangerous gang of aliens, as a protection against whom

the whole costly Immigration system is maintained
—voted solidly, in that debate, against the motion.
" You ask us," said the student, " to condemn
Capitalism for what it *has* done, and to approve
Communism for what it *will* do. The past we can
see with our own eyes : but the future we cannot :
we have to take it on trust from you, and we do
not see why we should."

With that argument the whole barracks con-
curred, and the motion, as I said, was defeated.

There were other reasons, however, besides my
refusal to fall into the clutches of a Bail Company,
why my detention was not very popular with the
Immigration officials. I had become too well
known a figure. News of my voyage had filled the
papers from one end of the country to the other :
and news of my present place of residence was not
altogether unknown to the public either. Where
it was known it was hardly welcome. One day
the Superintendent of the Barracks came to me in
a very uneasy frame of mind indeed. It seemed
that a press photographer had turned up, and
wanted to be allowed to photograph me behind bars.
In America, it seems, a press photographer can get
anywhere : it does not seem to have occurred to
the Superintendent to refuse the request outright :
he could only appeal to me. He felt sure, he said,
that such publicity would be highly unpleasant for

a man of my sensitive temperament : wasn't he right ? Surely I did not wish the photograph to be taken ? After all, a photograph like that would look as if I was in gaol : and this was not a gaol, it was only a kind of public hostelry where I was enjoying the hospitality of the State, and treated with the utmost consideration.

" It is gaol enough for me," I answered, " seeing I cannot get out." However, I saw what a jam the man was in and gave him my word that I did not wish the photograph taken.

However, it was plain that the authorities had learned their lesson, for in a few days I was given to understand that bail would not be insisted upon, and that I could leave on the personal recognizances of a responsible citizen. Influential friends —and I call them friends, though many of them were men I had never seen—had been at work on my behalf. So when the day of my adjourned hearing arrived I dropped the legal argument I had prepared and agreed to accept liberty on recognizances. Mr. Slavens McNutt, a scenario writer from Hollywood, went surety for me : and I was immediately released.

It so happened that I had been billed, long before my arrest, to speak that very evening at a Brotherhood Meeting of the First Presbyterian Church of

San Pedro, and I was now free to fulfil my engage-
ment. This I did. Another speaker that night
was my former gaoler, the Superintendent of the
San Pedro Barracks. Meeting again so soon like
this was a surprise to both of us : and to neither of
us, I think, a very comfortable one. He had his
work cut out in explaining away to the audience
the treatment meted out to another speaker on the
same platform. He regretted, he said, that they
had to detain me, but the law gave them no option.
He enlarged on the services of the Immigration
Department and dwelt on the magnanimity of the
officials who were now carrying out their strenuous
work on a reduced salary.

*   *   *

A few weeks later I read in the press that there
had been a clean-up in the San Pedro Immigration
Department : a few minor officials were dismissed
" for over zealousness in prosecuting their duty."
I was not sorry to feel that the light of publicity
which my case had let in on the workings of that
department had done some good.

However, I was not sorry either that my detention at their hands was now over—for the time
being at least.

CHAPTER XVII

California—Multiplicity of Sects—Hollywood—The Use of
Publicity—An Earthquake—I Join the " Holy Rollers "—
How I Earned My Living—Talk with the Preacher

BUT I had something else to do besides sampling
the hospitality of the American Immigration Department. My voyage, as I have said, was not complete.
My boat had come into port, yes : but my soul had
not.

California is alive with different religious sects :
this was a wonderful opportunity to sample them
all, and to find which one, if any, would answer
my needs. I was astounded at the number of
them : with so many religions in existence, there
hardly seemed any necessity for me to invent a
new one of my own. Surely one of them must
fit me.

Shortly after my first arrival I had been approached by an old-time sailor who was very
insistent that I should come to stay with him.
He said he had a large house all to himself in
Wilmington : that he would be glad of my com-

pany, and would charge me no rent. Wilmington seemed to be a quiet locality to live in : it was a good offer : so I accepted it, and stayed with him for nine months.

Meanwhile I had parted with the wreck of the *Elaine* : I sold it to a fellow-countryman for thirty-five dollars.

California is a strange country. At times I might have thought myself back in Australia : but not for long. Australian eucalyptus-trees and wattles lined the roads and avenues : but if I lifted my eyes to the distance, that was not Australian. Imagine a skyline which was a forest of oil wells : and beyond them, the sun-clad mountains. That skyline was not Australian : nor is there anything like it that I know of in the whole rest of the world.

The fame my voyage had won for me brought me, of course, invitations to Hollywood. I went. I was taken over studios, and introduced to famous film people. I would be standing beside some film beauty when, *click !*—and there would be another photograph for the press : " Fred Rebell showing his home-made sextant to Miss Blank," or something of the kind. Renowned actors and actresses, they were—to pose with whom was an honour for me, which I much appreciated.

All this publicity has since served me as a kind

of universal letter of introduction : wherever I go in the world, I generally come across somebody who has " read about me in the papers."

Another experience I had, almost as strange in its way as Hollywood, was an earthquake. It was not a bad one : but I had never experienced one before at all. I was sitting at supper when I heard a rumble as if a heavy steam-wagon were rushing past, and the whole room began to shake violently. My cup of cocoa spilt all over the table, and a few bottles fell off the pantry shelf : otherwise there was no damage in our house. But in the shopping centre it was a different story : windows smashed, walls cracked, bricks lying everywhere in the street. I believe there was a death-roll of seventy from that earthquake in that one county only.

Hollywood : an earthquake : and then America went off the Gold Standard. Once before, in Australia, I had lost forty per cent. of my savings that way. Now it happened again.

But neither Hollywood, nor the earthquake, nor the Gold Standard really mattered very deeply to me now ; for only half a block from where I was living in Wilmington I had found a public library ; and there I spent most of my time, in study. I ransacked the library shelves for books on psychic and religious matters, and devoured them whole. I read everything that seemed to throw any light

226

on the supernatural and the Hereafter, however unconventional : Psychic Science, Spiritualism, Black Magic, Eddyism, New Thought, Theosophy, Swedenborg, Mysticism, Occultism, Buddhism, Hinduism, Taoism, Mohammedanism—and every sect and heresy that had ever divided Christianity.

I read enough stuff there to bewilder most people : and much of it, of course, was contradictory : but on the other hand there was something which it all had in common. The body of evidence accumulated in all those books for the existence of the spiritual and the supernatural was so enormous that it quite outweighed in importance the contradictions. After reading it, it seemed incredible to me that anyone could be left in the world so bigoted as still to refuse to believe in God and the human soul, with such a mountain of evidence towering over him.

But when I wondered at that, I had only to reflect for how many years I had been such an unbeliever myself. I knew from my own case how it is that unbelief gets so sure a hold. Unbelief never encourages a man to look at the evidence and face it, and say honestly whether it convinces him or not : unbelief teaches him rather to nip past the evidence with his eyes shut. It is like a man who had a house near a mountain, but facing the other way. This man believed there was no mountain

227

behind his house . . . and so he never went round to the back of the house to look. For what was the good of looking if he knew there was no mountain there ? It would be simply a waste of time. That is the vicious circle in which unbelief lands you.

I did not, however, confine my exploring to books. I attended as many different churches and chapels as I was able ; for I knew that the Word of God was as likely to be a spoken as a written Word.

Frankly, in all the churches and chapels that I attended I found nothing new. One way or another they were professionals of religion : just carrying on with that little parcel of truth which they had been taught by their fathers and teachers, not looking for anything new, not searching for direct experience of God. But I wanted all or nothing. Once in my life, in a dream (as I have told you), I had felt the rays of the Love of God playing on my own very being : and I could not rest till I had found God with my waking mind also.

At last in my search I walked into a building which was announced as " Full Gospel Assembly." Had I known the reputation that building held in the neighbourhood, probably I would never have entered it ; for its congregation were mockingly known as " The Holy Rollers," and the sounds of their enthusiasm were so shocking to their neighbours that the neighbours had actually petitioned to have the place closed. However, I knew none of this, and walked in.

I saw at once that this place was in some way different. There was a tenseness in the atmosphere of the room : the singing was spirited : and it was followed by the testimony of various members of the congregation wherein they thanked God for salvation, for answering their prayers, for supplying their needs. For healing.

And for " the Baptism of the Holy Ghost."

The Baptism of the Holy Ghost ! That phrase kept recurring, and it set me thinking. Could it be that in fact *to-day* was still the Day of Pentecost ? That the Holy Ghost is still with us ?

Men know less of the Holy Ghost than they know of the other Persons of the Trinity. Why, when irreligious men swear blasphemous oaths you will notice that they swear by God the Father or God the Son : but you never hear them swear by God the Holy Ghost. This is not (as you may think) for fear of committing the unforgivable sin : for many of them are beyond the fear of committing any sin : it is simply that the Holy Ghost means nothing to them. They have heard of the Father, and of the Son : often in great detail : but of the Holy Ghost they know nothing whatever. They never think of Him.

Was it likely then that the Holy Ghost could still be at work unknown in this world ?

I was musing on this during the sermon. That sermon was no dry-as-dust theological dissertation or moral homily : no, the preacher seemed to have the gift for it, and preached like a house on fire. But what struck me most was not the preacher so much as the congregation. At emotional moments someone in the congregation would burst into utterance of words in a strange language—words which seemed to be in some way a comment on what the preacher was saying. Immediately after that another member of the congregation would stand up and interpret the words—and the message thus interpreted would be found to fit the sermon as a key fits a lock.

When the service was over the altar call was given : about half the congregation went and knelt at the altar rails to pray for twenty minutes or so. Some prayed aloud : some silently.

Can you wonder that I was interested ? I had felt during that service no working of the Holy Spirit in my own breast : I was there as an onlooker : but can you wonder that I thought " Here is something worth investigating " ?

They had about five services a week at that chapel, and I attended often. I studied the congregation and got to know many of them.

This congregation, I soon found, could be classed in three distinct divisions. First there were a few strangers like myself : men who were interested, but had no real part in what went on. The second class were the " saved." That is to say they had accepted Christ as their personal Saviour, and were slowly winning their way nearer to Him.

But it was the third class—about forty per cent. of the whole—in which I was most interested. These were they who made the supreme claim of all : that they had received the Baptism of the Holy Spirit, and having received it, they claimed to have won the battle against sin.

By that, don't think I mean that they never committed any sins, that they did as innocently as angels. The Tempter is old : the Tempter is wily : and the Tempter is always at work. No man is so saintly but that the Tempter will trip him from time to time into sinning. But there is a very real distinction between the man who sometimes sins, and the man whose distinguishing mark is that he is a sinner. The habitual sinner is chained to his sin : it has a hold on him : he likes it, and willingly sinks deeper into it. But the man who has conquered sin is the man on whom such sins as he may rarely commit *have no effect*. Like water which runs off a duck's back, and leaves it as dry as before, they leave his soul as innocent as it was.

I may have stressed this point too much and given you the impression that these people sinned as often as everyone else. That impression would be wrong : they lived, compared with the average man, the most exemplary lives. They had emotional and lovable natures. It was really the rarest thing for them to sin. All I mean to point out is that if one of them was occasionally deceived by the Tempter that did not for a moment weaken his claim to have won the victory over sin, or cast him back for ever from the Elect.

Now what interested me most about these people was their claim to have received the Baptism of the Holy Ghost exactly as you read of it in the Acts of the Apostles. I began to wonder if what they said was true—and if I too might some day hope to receive that Baptism.

Among the congregation there was a middle-aged lady, plain and below average height. I saw her there often with a Bible in her hands. One day, after the service, while some of the congregation were still praying at the altar rails and I was sitting in my seat reflecting upon what I had seen and listened to, I heard someone speak to me ; and saw this very lady standing in front of me.

" I perceive," she said, " that you are hungering after the Lord."

I looked at her : and as I looked at her, a strange transformation took place. Gone was this homely inconsiderable woman : in her place there stood before me a most beautiful angel. Words can but be beggared by the radiance and the glory of that vision : for in all this world I have seen nothing so beautiful. As a live person differs from a figure of clay, in such measure did this excellent vision transcend the lady who had just spoken to me.

I pulled myself together. What illusion could this be ? Was I dreaming ?—And once more I became aware of my surroundings ; of the lighted room, the row of seats in front of me. The vision faded away, and in its place I saw once more the woman, in her drab inconspicuous dress : with her wrinkled brow, kindly grey eyes, and plain un-powdered features.

She seemed wholly unaware of what I had seen in—or through—her. She was still speaking. She told me to keep on attending the assembly if I would find God : and learning that I was a stranger in the country, she invited me to her home.

I went. Frankly, I was interested in this woman who seemed to have an angel inside her. I wanted to know in what kind of environment she moved : how she lived. So I called at her home : and she introduced me to her husband, and to two of her sons aged 12 and 13. She had two other sons, I learned, both of them grown up : and one of them married.

They were all polite and attentive to me, but I discerned at once that they were not spiritually what this woman was. I asked her frankly : she told me it was true : that none of them but herself as yet were even " saved." She told me, more-over, that four years ago she had been in no better shape herself ; or rather, worse, for she had been the slave of an appalling temper. But then, dis-illusioned and despairing, she had gone down on her knees in the bathroom and stayed there until the Lord graciously heard and filled her with the Holy Spirit. From then on she knew that she was changed : she believed that when she died she would not have to face judgment, but would pass at once into life eternal.

But all this time, while I was (in that lady's phrase) " hungering after the Lord," I had bodily hunger to satisfy too. A man cannot live on air, and I had to support myself. The smashing of my boat by the naval launch now proved a blessing in disguise : for until my claim was settled one way or the other the Immigration Department could not banish me from the country. The wheels of government departments turn slowly, and it was many months and even years before a decision could be arrived at : before the American nation could decide whether or not to pay me the eighty-five dollars I asked.

In the meantime I worked. Beginning at my old trade of handyman I soon found myself in the role of a skilled yacht-builder : not that I built new yachts actually, but I did all kinds of work in old ones. I installed engines, tanks and stoves : I set port-lights and did yacht plumbing and carpentry work. One owner would recommend me to another ; and so long as I was in the States I never lacked work.

Now you will see that my spiritual progress was at this time in some ways at a standstill. It is easy to start upon the road to Salvation : but the way is long and hard. That is after all the first lesson taught by Bunyan's *Pilgrim's Progress*. You will remember how readily, when I first turned my thoughts towards God, my prayers had been answered : how storms had been quelled, clouds riven, everything given me that I asked for. But I was no longer content with praying for material things : and spiritual goods could not be had so readily.

But do not think that I had ceased praying for *material* things, or that such prayers had ceased to be answered. Far from it. Here is an example.

235

It so happened that some of the yacht work which I was given was far from Wilmington : and I had to get there somehow. Nearly everyone in California has a car, but I had none. Seeing that my stay there was so precarious, I was not willing to risk any large part of my savings in buying myself a vehicle that perhaps I should be unable to sell again when suddenly commanded to leave. Ten dollars was the utmost I could afford to pay : and the most I could hope, for that sum, was a T-model Ford.

However, I found none at the price I wanted : so I prayed for one. The very next day I saw such a car for sale : and the price, incredible though this may seem, was *three* dollars ! Less than the cost of a new tyre. I bought that car : it served me well : there was nothing wrong with it.

But I did not seem able to come any nearer to receiving the Baptism of God the Holy Ghost.

I still attended many different chapels—I did not only go to the Full Gospel Assembly, or Pentecostal Church. I had at this time moved my habitation : I was living at a hotel now. The owner of this hotel was himself among the " saved " : he had been a bootlegger, and he had served a term in gaol ; but with the help of Christian missioners he had been changed, and now for over ten years had trodden the straight and narrow path. With

236

this man I would often drive round to distant churches and chapels in the district : for I could not relax my search for an unnecessary instant. Mostly, however, it was to meeting-places of the Pentecostal type that I went : the " Full Gospel," the " Four Square," the " Holiness," the " Bethel-Temple," and others like them. Up till now I had thought that the number of people in the world who had received this Baptism of the Holy Spirit must be very small ; and I was surprised to learn that their number is estimated at about fifteen million.

This Baptism of the Holy Ghost is a single experience, by which a man's life is changed for ever after ; and it does not need to be repeated : but when those who have been thus baptized meet together as the Early Christians did, they receive further " infillings " of the Spirit, again as the Early Christians did. With these " infillings " come the same gifts that we read about in the Bible : the power to speak in strange tongues—not gibberish, but real foreign languages, often Oriental : powers of divination and prophecy : and the power of Apostolic leadership. How was it, you might well ask, if people had these miraculous powers, that they did not use them for commercial or at least publicizing ends ? The answer is simple : in the first place they had no wish to : in the second, if they had had that wish the power would have immediately deserted them.

* * *

At length, however, I grew tired of being an onlooker, however devout. Impatient that the gift of the Holy Spirit was withheld from me for so long I spoke to the pastor about it, and he put his finger on the trouble at once. Disbelief was in me still : I sought this Baptism of the Holy Spirit *in order that at last I might finally and wholly believe.* But that was the wrong way round. Until I could finally and wholly believe, I should never obtain the Baptism of the Holy Spirit ! That Baptism is something too precious to be used merely as evidence, or to cleanse the soul from doubt. Only the soul from which doubt has been finally banished is fit to receive it.

Then I saw that the road in front of me was still a long one : for by nature I have a doubting and sceptical mind, and on top I have been cursed with education. Did I believe in the Bible, the pastor asked me ?

" Yes," said I, " substantially I do."

" Substantially is not enough," he answered. " You must believe in it unreservedly and wholly."

" How can I be positive that the Bible is the true Word of God, when I know for a fact that it has been written down by erring men ?

" As the proof of the pudding is in the eating," said the Pastor, " so the proof of the Bible is in its operation. You have now been long enough watching and observing fervent Christian circles to know that on the strength of the Bible sinners receive salvation, burdens are lifted, drunkards and criminals are changed into respectable citizens, incurable diseases are healed, prayers are being answered, and the saints are being filled with spirit and power. Where else can you find a creed that gives you half as much ? Your difficulty is an oversceptical mind. Religion is essentially a matter of the heart, of purpose, or the will, and you must not let an overcritical reason hamper and handicap that will. The Lord has consideration for doubting Thomases, too. He will never leave or forsake you now, and will satisfy you eventually, if you continue to seek Him, for the Lord is more willing to give good gifts to us than we are to our children."

" But how can I resign my reason and implicitly believe in the Bible, if it is patent to me that this, that and the other thing have been misstated in it or misrepresented, or is contradictory."

" You should not make mountains out of mole-hills. There are no contradictions in the Bible, and the same doctrine runs from cover to cover. Whatever little discrepancies of reportership or detail there may be, it certainly does not pay to quibble over them. Besides, at your age, you might show more discrimination between friend and foe. I am positive that you are well enough acquainted with the saints to know that they wish you good, materially, bodily and spiritually, that they love you, and would share their last morsel of bread with you ; then why do you doubt their testimony ? Most of them have gone through similar or identical mental and spiritual stress to what you have been in, and they have come through rejoicing, so why then not take their advice ? Why not believe them when they tell you that they have found the Bible true, and Christ's promises far more dependable than any pledge of nations, and far more secure than the strongest bank vault ever built. Why give more credence to the opinion of some atheist or higher critic, who professes interest in your material welfare, yet would never give a drat if you hung yourself to-morrow ? You also desire to have the Baptism first, that you may believe afterwards, but such is not God's way of dealing with His children. He desires that we should have trust and confidence in Him, as in a loving father, and that we should believe in His word as stated in the Bible. Therefore to such of His children as expect and believe Him to supply their needs, and to answer their prayers—He grants their requests quickly, whilst others, that have not the same confidence in God, but just keep on cadging of Him—may have to wait a long time before they get what they ask. His Word says : ' Whatsoever you desire, when you pray—believe that you receive it—and you shall have it.' Through unbelief in God's Word the human race has fallen, and only by believing and obeying it can we again climb the steps to heavenly glory."

" But if I have to believe first, and expect the thing to come about afterwards, what assurance can I have that the ' Baptism of the Spirit ' is not merely a figment of my imagination, or the result of auto-suggestion ? "

" I know of thousands of authentic cases where by trusting and obeying the Word of God people have obtained peace of mind, riddance from vice, deliverance from disease, answer to prayer, joy unspeakable and supernatural gifts, but I do not know of a single instance where any of these results have been brought about by ' auto-suggestion.' That term has been coined by unbelievers, who try to explain spiritual phenomena in a natural way. Believe me, that when you cast all your doubts aside, lay a wholehearted trust in the Bible, and apply all of your will to seek the Baptism of the Holy Spirit—you most certainly will receive the infilling, and you will know it for a fact that you have it."

"Well," said I, "that was quite a sermon : it fits me, and with God's help it shall guide me."

CHAPTER XVIII

*Two and a Half Years in California : My Boast Fulfilled—
Arrested Again—The Deportation Barracks—American
Prisons—Sex Perversion and Religiosity—Deported from
the United States—My Home-coming—Nostalgia for the
Pacific—" Go, Little Book ! "*

IT took the American Government two and a half
years to decide on paying me the eighty-five dollars
I demanded for damage to my boat ! So I spent
two and a half years in California, thus fulfilling
the boast (or prophecy) that I had made to the
American Consul in Sydney, when I told him that
I would go to America without a visa, and stay
there as long as I liked. By now I was growing
anxious to return to the country of my birth, and
to see my old parents once more before they died.
So I wrote to the Immigration Department, telling
them that my claim had been settled—which was
the equivalent of telling them that they were now
free to deport me.

On the 8th October, 1935, I was busy working on a big pleasure-yacht, when up drove the
Black Maria with two officers from the Immi-

gration Department inside. They gave me only
a couple of hours in which to pack up and get
ready for deportation. When I complained that
they ought to have given me longer notice,
they replied somewhat sarcastically that I had
had two and a half years in which to pack my
grip.

They drove me once more to the San Pedro
Barracks, and there I was kept under lock and key
for two weeks : so they need not have been in such
a hurry. During these two weeks many of my
friends came to bid me farewell : and were surprised to find me so calm and happy under what
seemed to them the terrible misfortune of having
to leave America.

Many of my fellow deportees, it is true, were far
from happy. But generally this was due not so
much to sorrow at leaving America as apprehension
at what awaited them where they were bound.
One of them, for instance, was a man born of English
parentage in Mexico : he was suspected now of
having taken part in a Mexican revolution, and if
he was sent back there would certainly be stood
up against a wall.

Another Britisher had been resident in the United
States for seven years. He innocently paid a visit
to Canada, and after it was refused re-entry. Somehow he managed to get back to his former home :

but only to be arrested and dispatched to San Pedro to wait deportation with the rest of us. Another of the deportees, on the other hand, might be described as a " habitual." He was a Mexican whose family lived in California. He was slippery as an eel, and every time that they pushed him across the frontier he was back in California almost before the Immigration Officer was home himself. He had served five gaol sentences for this, but nothing seemed to deter him, or indeed have any effect on him : and I have no doubt that just as water wears away stone, so in the end the American Government will have to forget about him and let him stay.

Another lad had given the authorities endless trouble : they could not discover his real name and nationality, although they believed him to be a Canadian. So there was nowhere they could send him to. Every kind of ruse failed to get the information from him, until at last they struck a successful one. One of the officers pretended to take a great liking for the lad and finally offered to adopt him. Once adopted, he was told, he would then be an American citizen. But for the adoption to be legal his new father *must* know who his parents really were. Poor young Willie fell for the ruse at last, and gave up his secret. His parents were Canadians : and so he was bundled over the Canadian frontier before you could say knife.

At last the day came, and we embarked on the three days' train-journey across Arizona and Texas to Galveston on the Gulf of Mexico.

But the American Government, it seemed, was not tired of our company yet ; and instead of being shipped at once, at Galveston we were locked up in a barracks yet again.

Amongst our new companions in this barracks were many ex-convicts ; and once again I had an opportunity to learn about a side of American life that I should not have met with in Society or the Lecture hall.

I learnt as much about the American prison system as I could. Now it is quite plain, from what I was told, that the system is on the whole good. The food is good, the discipline strict, the punishment no worse than deserved, and opportunities for learning a trade are provided. Yet the results don't tally. None of this seems to have the desired effect. It is seldom indeed that the criminal is reformed and starts a new life.

The reason for this, I believe, is a very simple and purely practical one. However hard the prisoner works at the trade he learns in gaol, *he is not allowed to earn any money at it*. This cannot be logically defended : it is the tyranny of the Trades Unions which imposes it against the Government's better judgment.

If the prisoner felt that some of the work he was doing was building up a nest-egg for him, which would help him to make a new start when he left prison, he would work with far more of a will— and be a respectable monied man by the time his sentence was served. But instead of that, he is thrown out penniless into a friendless world, having learned little of his trade in prison except the ability to shirk.

Is it surprising then if he drifts back into his old ways, and starts to make his living once more by the devious means which alone he really knows ?

I asked one ex-convict if there were no Christian missionaries in the prisons, no chance for religion to soften the criminal's heart.

" No," he said : " the Salvation Army come on Sundays : but no one takes much notice of them. And such few professing Christians as you find in a prison are seldom a credit to their religion. Most commonly they are senile old men doing long sentences for sexual offences against children and minors."

For such cases as those, indeed, nothing could be worse than the American prison system which locks up two or four *men* in a single cell with little or nothing to think about except each other. Naturally sex perversion is rampant—or so my informant told me.

" But you mean to say," said I, " that such a state of things is tolerated by the prison administration ? "

" Why not ? " was his equable reply. " It is not only tolerated but encouraged. What kind of hope lies before an old man serving a long sentence ? He has no future to look forward to : he must live in the present. Without this sexual indulgence he would become cantankerous, suicidal, or dangerous. But as things are the warder can always exert pressure on him by taking away his ' girl ' till he behaves himself. Therefore the system works to the advantage of both parties : the gaolers and their boarders as well !—However, those few individuals who insistently refuse to get ' married ' are known to the warders and left severely alone."

As written matter is not allowed to be taken out of gaol it was interesting to hear of the commissions and messages which the released men had been entrusted with, to carry to the dear ones of their prison friends. Naturally, all these messages had to be memorized. But alas ! very few of the released men ever keep their promises to their prison friends. After all, if they were men of honesty or moral principle the odds are they would never have got into gaol in the first place.

I spent seventeen days in the barracks at Galveston , and then at last was embarked, with two German ex-sailors and one Swede, on the S.S. *Chester Valley*, bound with a cargo of cotton for Bremen.

The crossing took twenty-two days, and we landed on 2nd December. At Bremen I was provided with railway tickets to Riga, and arrived there two days later.

It was touching to compute how much money the Federal Government must have spent on me, one way or another. At a moderate estimate they must have squandered at least three hundred dollars of public money : whereas if they had left me at peace I should have cost them nothing.

*　　　*　　　*

The fame and honour which the American press had accorded me had even reached Latvia. The stories of my voyage had been copied in the Latvian papers, and the country was prepared to be proud of me : there was talk of public luncheons and all sorts of things. But when the returning hero arrived a deportee, the bouquets were hurriedly put back in their cardboard boxes, and the receptions called off! This was fortunate for me, as I was enabled to do what I wanted—to go home in peace and quiet.

How happily I had dreamed of the homeland in my moments of home-sickness! Had conjured up before my inward eye visions of wintry landscapes, of snow and bare, wind-swept boughs! But how different it all seemed now that I was actually there: and how very cold the winter felt after twenty-eight years in Australia and California! Never can a returning exile have shivered so mightily as I did on my first arrival in Latvia.

Moreover, like the aftermath of some devastating storm, I saw everywhere the marks and scars of the World War. The rich had grown poor: whole families had been wiped out of existence. The death-roll in Latvia had been appalling: some forty per cent. of the adult male population. And yet, when I returned to my native town of Windau how little at first seemed changed! There were still the old flag-stone side-walks, the cobbled streets: the old houses (a little dingier and more dilapidated): the same old lanes and by-ways. What memories they brought back into my mind of people I had known: of youthful loves and fancies! When I looked at the streets of the town I felt that I had come home: but when I looked at the faces in those streets I knew I was a stranger. At one time almost every face I passed would have been familiar . . . now there was not a single face that I recognized, or that recognized me.

I hired a horse-cab to drive to Pilten, for I learned that my parents had acquired a farm there.

It was a drive of seventeen or eighteen miles, and I did not get there till dusk. I saw a tottering old man shuffling out of the barn : could that be my father ? Well, he answered to the name.

What is it I am saying, he asks ? His son Paul from America ? Oh, Heavens, can that be true ?

Yes, true enough ! Next moment we were round each other's necks. And questions ! But he pulls himself up and says, " Go into the house. Mother sure will be glad : we have often been speaking about you, wondering when you would come."

*   *   *

Quietly passes the winter, spring, and summer under the parental roof. But when the chilly blasts of autumn had begun to yellow the foliage : and when, high up, the birds of passage were taking their departure in clamorous droves, a restless feeling came over my soul. Regretfully I had been watching, for days, the sun's diminishing arc in the sky—before I realized that the *wander-lust* had me again in its grip, and that I too must away.

My heart longed to be there, where the life-giving sun had flown : where everything was abloom and fragrant. I knew that the longer I stayed in Latvia, the more my misery would increase. I thought of the lovely Pacific islands ; and I felt the sea in my blood, stirring. In fancy I could see myself sailing the seas once more in a little boat, and hear the lapping of wavelets against her bow.

For somewhere in the broad Pacific there is an enchanting island, where the gentle " Trade " rustles in the tree-tops. There, on the coral shore beside the emerald lagoon, stands a lovely maiden. She gazes longingly out to sea, hoping to observe some day a white sail rise above the horizon, a little boat come into view, bearing her the hero-sailor whom she fancies best.—Yes, somewhere in the Pacific there is an English maid, fair as the lily, bright as the morning star : and in spite of my shortcomings she loves me best. Five years have flown by, with their testings and trials : hearts have grown cold, and memories faint : but one heart I know still beats loyal and true, one dearest friend still is longing for me.

She shall not have to wait much longer : for of a certainty I shall sail again soon, to claim my prize and my love. Then I trust that the two of us will spend the rest of our lives in loving one another, and in the service of the King of Kings. For happiness indeed is to be found in loving and being loved : but it can never excel, nor last, nor endure, unless we love God above all.

Dear reader, if you have no peace of mind, if the world gives you no lasting satisfaction and its pleasures turn to ashes in your mouth, if you are sick and tired, then this is the first step for you to take : ask some fervent and believing Christian to pray for the peace of your soul. Your path thereafter may be awfully rough : but peace of soul will come to you in the end. It is far easier for the rankest criminal, murderer, or sinner to be reborn, to receive a change of heart and to become a different man than for the sceptic, the materialist, or the evolutionist. Yet even he, as I have found, can win peace in the end.

Should old Foxy Brian see me now, I am sure he would say : " Well, well ! There is another good man gone crazy over religion. Very nice to talk to, mind you, but unquestionably a religious maniac."

But what do I care ! If I am mad, it is a good kind of madness with me.

*   *   *

Go, little book. Already thou hast been rejected by a number of publishers, nor did an agent have any better luck with thee. The market for manuscripts is glutted. There is no *reason* whatever why thy fortune should change. But Thou, O God of Heaven, art able to change circumstances ! I care neither for publicity, fame, nor renown : and money matters to me little, for Thou O Lord art amply providing for my needs. Nevertheless, if there be one soul astray in the Valley of Despair who by reading my story might take courage, and by following in my tracks might find peace and rest, then, O Lord, Grant that my book be printed.